Artificial Intelligence - Scope and Limitations

Edited by Dinesh G. Harkut

Published in London, United Kingdom

IntechOpen

Supporting open minds since 2005

Artificial Intelligence - Scope and Limitations
http://dx.doi.org/10.5772/intechopen.77611
Edited by Dinesh G. Harkut

Contributors
Suk Lee, Eunbin Ju, Chul Yong Kim, Suk Woo Choi, Hyungju Lee, Jang Bo Shim, Kyung Hwan Chang, Kwang Hyeon Kim, Yuanjie Cao, Cristobal Fernandez-Robin, Diego Yañez, Scott McCoy, Ramoni Lasisi, Robert DuPont, Valentina Talimonchik, Dinesh G. Harkut, Kashmira Kasat

First published in London, United Kingdom, 2019 by IntechOpen
IntechOpen is the global imprint of INTECHOPEN LIMITED, registered in England and Wales, registration number: 11086078, The Shard, 25th floor, 32 London Bridge Street
London, SE19SG - United Kingdom
Printed in Croatia

British Library Cataloguing-in-Publication Data
A catalogue record for this book is available from the British Library

Additional hard copies can be obtained from orders@intechopen.com

Artificial Intelligence - Scope and Limitations
Edited by Dinesh G. Harkut
p. cm.
Print ISBN 978-1-78985-935-5
Online ISBN 978-1-78985-936-2

Meet the editor

Dr. Dinesh G. Harkut is currently working as an associate professor at PRMCEAM, Badnera, India in the Computer Science & Engineering Department. He obtained his Bachelors, Masters of Engineering Degree (CSE), and PhD (CSE) from SGBAU Amravati University, Maharashtra, India. He also holds a Masters and a PhD in business administration. His primary research interests are in computer AI, big data, analytics, embedded systems, and e-commerce. He supervised around 18 Masters Degree and 24 Bachelors Degree Students. He has published forty papers in refereed journals and three books with international publishers. He has two patents filed and published in his name in India and has organized various workshops, sessions, conferences, and training sessions. He is a principal investigator in centers of excellence of renowned technological giants such as: IBM, Oracle, Texas Instruments, and Huawei at PRMCEAM and establishing industry-funded laboratories at ARM, Cypress Semiconductor, Intel FPGA, Wind River. For Xilinx he obtained a grant of Rs. 351.32 lacs.
He has a Fellow of the Institute of Electronics & Telecommunication Engineering (IETE), New Delhi. He is a Life Member of the Indian Society for Technical Education (ISTE), New Delhi, a Senior Member of the Universal Association of Computer and Electronics Engineers (UACEE) USA, and Professional Member of the International Association of Engineers (IAENG), Hong Kong.

Contents

Preface

The thing that's going to make artificial intelligence so powerful is its ability to learn, and the way AI learns is to look at human culture.

—Dan Brown

This book comprehensively introduces artificial intelligence (AI). While it has been studied for decades, it still remains a potent buzzword and one of the most abstract subjects in computer science. It is a science and a set of computational techniques inspired by the way in which human beings use their nervous system and their body to feel, learn, reason, and act. AI is already an intrinsic part of our daily life and has greatly impacted the lifestyle of every human being. Every emerging technology is a source of both enthusiasm and skepticism. AI has both advantages and disadvantages, depending on one's perspective. The material is presented in a clear, simple style and encompasses many challenges and opportunities in the fascinating area of AI.

We would like to convey our appreciation to all contributors, including the accepted chapters' authors. Our special thanks go to Ms. Lada Bozic, Author Service Manager IntechOpen, London, UK for her kind support and great efforts in bringing the book to fruition. In addition, we also appreciate all those who worked in the background and assisted in formatting the book.

Dr. Dinesh G. Harkut
Associate Professor,
Dept. of Computer Science & Engineering,
Prof Ram Mehge College of Engineering & Management,
Badnera-Amravati, M.S., India

Chapter 1

Introductory Chapter: Artificial Intelligence - Challenges and Applications

Dinesh G. Harkut, Kashmira Kasat and Vaishnavi D. Harkut

1. What is artificial intelligence (AI)?

Artificial intelligence (AI) is any task performed by program or machine, which otherwise human needs to apply intelligence to accomplish it. It is the science and engineering of making machines to demonstrate intelligence especially visual perception, speech recognition, decision-making, and translation between languages like human beings. AI is the simulation of human intelligence processes by machines, especially computer systems. This includes learning, reasoning, planning, self-correction, problem solving, knowledge representation, perception, motion, manipulation, and creativity. It is a science and a set of computational techniques that are inspired by the way in which human beings use their nervous system and their body to feel, learn, reason, and act. AI is related to machine learning and deep learning wherein machine learning makes use of algorithms to discover patterns and generate insights from the data they are working on. Deep learning is a subset of machine learning, one that brings AI closer to the goal of enabling machines to think and work as human as possible.

AI is a debatable topic and is often represented in a negative way; some would call it a blessing in disguise for businesses, while for some it is a technology that endangers the mere existence of humankind as it is potentially capable of taking over and dominating human being, but in reality artificial intelligence has affected our lifestyle either directly or indirectly and shaping the future of tomorrow. AI has already become an intrinsic part of our daily life and has greatly impacted our lifestyle despite the imperative uses of digital assistants of mobile phones, driver-assistance systems, the bots, texts and speech translators, and systems that assist in recommending products and services and customized learning.

Every emerging technology is a source of both enthusiasm and skepticism. AI is a source of both advantages and disadvantages in different perspectives. However, we need to overcome certain challenges before we can realize the true potential and immense transformational capabilities of this emerging technology. Some of the challenges related to artificial intelligence are:

2. Challenges

Building trust: The AI is all about science, technology, and algorithms which mostly people are unaware of, which makes it difficult for them to trust it.

AI human interface: Being a new technology, there is a huge shortage of working manpower having data analytics and data science skills; those in turn can be deputed to get maximum output from artificial intelligence. As the advancement of

AI rising, businesses lack a skilled professional who can match the requirement and work with this technology. Business owners need to train their professionals to be able to leverage the benefits of this technology.

Investment: AI is an expensive technology that not every business owner or manager can invest money into as large amount of computing power will be necessary and sometimes hardware acceleration with GPU, FPGA, or ASIC must be in place to run machine learning models effectively. Though adoptability of AI is surging high, it has not been integrated fully in business's value chain at the scale which it should have. Moreover, enterprises of those who have incorporated are still in nascent stage which have resulted in the slowdown in the lifting of the AI technology at scale and thus been deprived of cost benefit of scale. After decades of speculation and justifiable anxiety about the social implications of intensifying & potentially de-stabilizing AI technology for humankind and Black box problem, AI investors are bit skeptical from parking their money in potential startups.

Software malfunction: With machines and algorithms controlling AI, decision-making ability is automatically ceded to code-driven Black Box tools. Automation makes it difficult to identify the cause of mistakes and malfunctions. Moreover, due to the lack of ability of human beings to learn and understand how these tools work, they have little or no control over the system which is further complicated as automated systems become more prevalent and complex.

Non-invincible: (Can replace only certain tasks) Like any other technology, AI also has its own limitations; it simply cannot replace all tasks. However, it will result in emerging new job domain with different quality job profile.

High expectations: Research in artificial intelligence is conducted by large pool of technologist and scientists with varying objectives, motivation perspectives, and interests. Main focus of research is confined in understanding the underlying basis of cognition and intelligence with heavy emphasis on unraveling the mysteries of human intelligence and thought process. Not everyone understands the functioning of AI and might also have very high expectation of functioning.

Data security: Machine learning and decision-making capability of AI and AI application are based on huge volumes of classified data, often sensitive and personal in nature. This makes it vulnerable to serious issues like data breach and identity theft. Mostly, companies and government striving for profits and power, respectively, exploit the AI-based tools which are generally globally networked which make them difficult to regulate or rein in.

Algorithm bias: AI is all about data and algorithms. Accuracy of decision-making capability of AI is purely based on how accurately it has been trained and by using authentic and unbiased data. Unethical and unfair consequences are inherent in vital decision-making if data used for training is laced with racial, gender, communal, or ethnic biases. Such biases will probably be more accentuated, as many AI systems will continue to be trained using bad data.

Data scarcity: Power and capabilities of AI and AI applications depend directly on the accuracy and relevancy of supervised and labeled datasets being used for training and learning. There is scarcity of quality-labeled data. Though efforts are underway by means of transfer learning, active learning, deep learning, and unsupervised learning, to devise methodologies to make AI models learn despite the scarcity of quality-labeled data, it will only aggravate the problem.

3. Application domain

Artificial neural networks allow modeling of nonlinear processes and become a useful tool for solving many problems such as classification, clustering, dimension reduction, regression, structured prediction, machine translation, anomaly detection, pattern recognition, decision-making, computer vision, visualization, and others. This wide range of abilities makes it possible to use artificial neural networks in many areas. Recent developments in AI techniques complimented by the availability of high computational capacity at increasingly accessible costs, wide availability of labeled data, and improvement in learning techniques result in exploring the wide application domain for AI. Anticipated progress of AI is shown in **Figure 1**.

AI improves lives of human beings by assisting in driving, taking personal care of aged /handicap people, executing arduous and dangerous tasks, assisting in making informed decisions, rationally managing huge amounts of data that would otherwise be difficult to interpret, assisting in translating, and communicating multilingually while not knowing the language of our interlocutors and many more.

Artificial intelligence is already everywhere and is widely used in ways that are quite obvious. Some of the areas currently on the priority list include but not limited to:

Collaborative systems: Research on collaborative systems investigates models and algorithms to support the development of autonomous systems that can collaborate with each other and with human beings.

Computer vision: Till the advent of computer vision, support-vector machines were considered the most used method for visual classification activities and were the most relevant form of machine perception. Further, deep learning has deep impact on computer vision which is complimented by the evolution and low-cost availability of large-scale computing and the availability of large amounts of data. Moreover, the fine-tuning of networks of neural network algorithms has allowed the AI to perform visual classification tasks better than human beings.

Crowd sourcing and human computation: It is focused on the creation of innovative ways to exploit human intelligence.

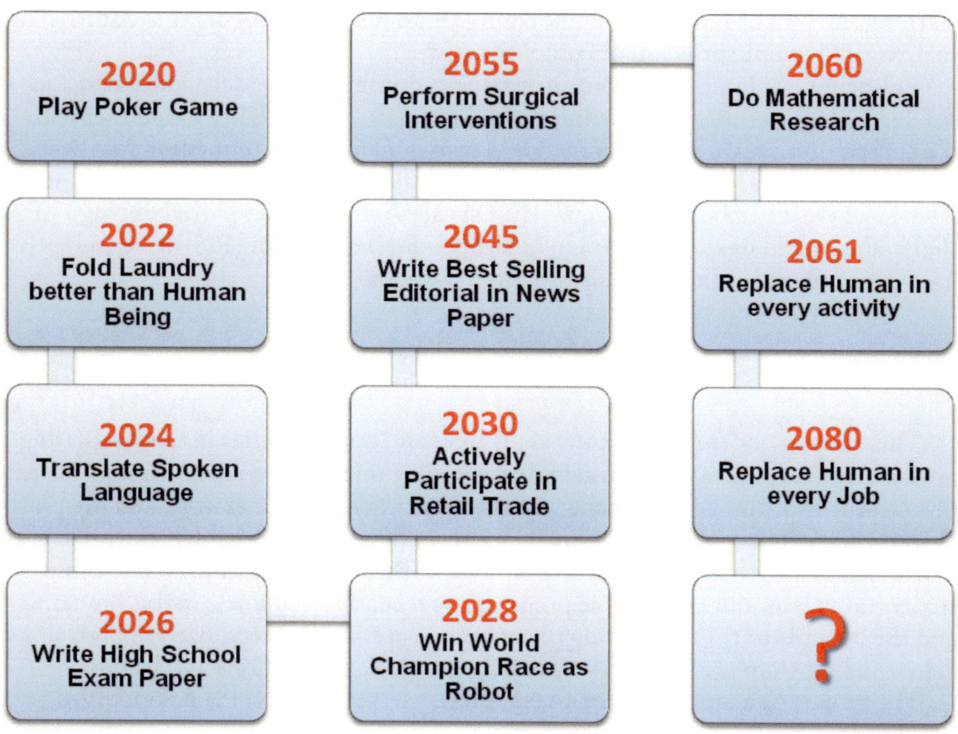

Figure 1.
Anticipated progress of artificial intelligence.

Deep learning (DL): The ability to learn convolutional neural networks has brought many benefits to the computer vision sector, with applications such as object recognition, video labeling, and other variants.

Internet of things (IoT): Artificial intelligence plays a growing role in IoT applications and deployments. The value of AI in this context is its ability to quickly wring insights from data. Moreover, machine learning brings the ability to automatically identify patterns and detect anomalies in the data that smart sensors and devices generate. Other AI technologies such as speech recognition and computer vision can help extract insight from data that used to require human review. AI plays a growing role in IoT applications and deployments and is making a big splash in the Internet of things.

Machine learning (ML): Many basic problems in machine learning (such as supervised and non-supervised learning) are well known. A central focus in current studies concerns the chance of increasing the ability of algorithms to work on extremely large datasets.

Natural language processing (NLP): It is a very dynamic sector in the area of machine perception which is majorly associated with automatic speech recognition. It is nothing but imparting the ability to understand human language as it is spoken to computer program. Research in this area is basically focused on the ability to develop systems capable of interacting with people through dialog and not with simple standard reactions which find application in enterprise search which involves organized retrieval of structured and unstructured data within an organization.

Neuromorphic computing: Traditional computers use von Neumann's architecture model. With the success of the deep neural networks, alternative models are being developed, many of which are inspired by neural biological networks.

Reinforcement learning: Through rule extraction, pattern matching, and mining, machine learning become one of the important tools which is further complimented by motivational decision-making capability implemented via reinforcement learning. Advent of reinforcement learning sharpens the ability of AI to address the real-world dynamic problem of complex nature.

Robotics: Navigation of robots in static environments is widely addressed and resolved. Now studies are revolving around exploring their ability to interact with the surrounding reality in a predictable way in dynamic environment in real time.

This is just a partial list of exhaustive application domain area of artificial intelligence where it can be used extensively. One area which was explored during PhD thesis, illustrated next, is the design of fuzzy inference system (FIS)-based adaptive hardware task scheduler for multiprocessor systems.

4. Conclusion

This chapter encompasses many challenges and opportunities in the fascinating area of AI. AI is playing an increasingly important role in our society. Though it has been learnt and studied for decades, it still remains a strong buzzword and the most abstract subject in computer science. Until recently, it has been mostly the topic of discussion among science fiction writers and worked on; it was confined to university research labs, but remarkable progress has recently been made in this domain, and the benefits of this happening phenomenon are widely recognized in diversified areas ranging from medicine to security to consumer applications and business.

The impact of adaptive neuro-fuzzy inference system (ANFIS) has emerged as a dominant technique for addressing highly nonlinear, complex, and dynamic research problems which required cognitive skills. The ability of machines to demonstrate the application of this advanced cognitive skills in predicting behavior, decision-making, language processing (written or spoken), and learning (supervised or unsupervised) makes this domain of paramount importance in today's world which is highly influenced by massive volume of unsupervised data. Exponential growth of data generation, sophisticated storage capabilities, steady increases of computing power, and advancement in research machine self-learning have greatly enhanced the capabilities of AI.

There are pros and cons of every new disruptive technology, and AI is no exception to this rule. AI has implications for privacy, data protection, and the rights of individuals which pose social and ethical challenges which are further exaggerated by self-learning algorithms gaining controls of societies and people. Many people are expressing their anxiety and predicting that the havoc which AI could wreak may be in terms of growing deluge of unemployment and disenchantments. However, AI revolution will create plenty of new data science, machine learning, engineering, and IT job positions to develop and maintain the systems and software that will be running those AI algorithms and enhance the quality of life of mankind.

Author details

Dinesh G. Harkut[1*], Kashmira Kasat[2] and Vaishnavi D. Harkut[1]

1 Department of Computer Science and Engineering, Prof Ram Meghe College of Engineering and Management, Amravati, India

2 Department of Electronics and Telecommunication Engineering, Prof Ram Meghe College of Engineering and Management, Amravati, India

*Address all correspondence to: dg.harkut@gmail.com

Chapter 2

Intention to Use WhatsApp

Cristobal Fernández-Robin, Diego Yáñez and Scott McCoy

Abstract

More than 1.8 billion people use WhatsApp nowadays, out of which 70% uses it daily. In this scenario, this study seeks modeling the variables that positively influence the intention to use WhatsApp. To this end, 579 surveys based on the unified theory of acceptance and use of technology are conducted. The descriptive results show that individuals use WhatsApp mainly motivated by leisure. In this sense, according to the structural equation model, the variable with the greatest influence on behavioral intention is hedonic motivation, followed by social influence, performance expectancy, and effort expectancy. These results indicate that most people use WhatsApp principally because they find it fun, enjoyable, and very entertaining, something more inherent to an entertainment application than to a messaging application. Nevertheless, a cluster analysis indicates the existence of two consumer segments: one showing a certain indifference and disagreement regarding the usefulness of WhatsApp for their activities and duties and the other manifesting that it uses WhatsApp not only for leisure but also for work, academic, and informative reasons. These differences in consumer drivers might have a great impact on WhatsApp and its competition marketing strategies.

Keywords: WhatsApp, social computing, leisure, social network, mobile apps

1. Introduction

It has become increasingly common to see people interacting with their smartphones while performing other activities at any time and place. There are millions of applications that can be used to keep in contact with family and friends, order food, take a taxi, book a hotel, set up a blind date, or simply to be reachable at work. However, despite this wide variety of applications and content to be created and visited, it is not surprising that most of the time spent on the phone is destined to the use of social networks. According to [1], smartphone, along with its cousin, tablet and a fast-expanding family of wearables and other smart devices are transforming the way people live, work, play, connect, and interact. Martin [2] suggests that the time spent in the digital world on mobile devices such as smartphones and tablets is longer than the time spent on traditional devices such as computers and laptops, in some countries like Indonesia or India, where the use of smartphones and tablets accounts for 90% of the time spent on digital media. Undoubtedly, this is due to a greater access to these devices, with increasingly cheaper purchasing options and better features, to the extent that today these technologies can perfectly replace laptops for many people. Additionally, another factor that indeed played an important role in the increased use of mobile devices is mobile apps. In this sense, we can confirm that mobile devices definitely changed digital entertainment.

The influence of mobile apps is evidenced by the fact that their use represents more than 90% of the time spent on smartphones and tablets, with Latin American countries on the top of the list: Argentina (94%), Mexico (92%), and Brazil (89%). In addition, mobile devices are used more than traditional devices like computers to access the digital world. This behavior is common in users of all ages, but it is more concentrated in women [2]. Regarding the reach of mobile apps, the app universe is dominated by a small group, with 96% of the time spent on no more than 10 apps [2], most of them corresponding to social networks such as Facebook, Instagram, and WhatsApp.

In connection, according to Smith [3], Facebook has more than 2.234 billion active users per month. Sixty-six percent of these users use the app daily, out of which 51% visit it several times per day, which translates to more than 2 trillion posts and 1.13 trillion likes since the launch of the app.

Another popular social network is Instagram. This app has 1 billion active users per month. Twenty-two percent of them use it daily, out of which 38% check the app multiple times during the day [3].

For its part, WhatsApp, a free app that offers messaging and calls in a simple, safe, and reliable way to phones all over the world, has more than 1.8 billion active users. Seventy percent of them use the app daily, which translates into 65 billion messages sent, 100 million voice calls, and 55 million video calls per day [3].

These data seem to indicate that the use of WhatsApp is more intensive than other popular social networks, even though it is not the most popular social network, and some people could categorize it as a messaging application instead of a social network. In view of this, the research question that arises is what makes users prefer this social network? Is an attractive proposal and design enough to capture a large quantity of people, or there is something else in play? Is it only on the users to decide what social networks will be used? This study seeks to answer these questions, specifically regarding the intention to use WhatsApp and using an adaptation of the technology acceptance model known as UTAUT2 to achieve this goal [4].

2. Development

2.1 Background

Created as an extension to the world of the theory of reasoned action [5], the technology acceptance model [6] corresponds to one of the most renowned, analyzed, and studied models in the literature. This model seeks to understand how and why users accept and use a technology, using perceived ease of use and perceived usefulness as prediction variables of the intention to use. TAM2 was created after TAM and explains the intentions to use a specific technology in terms of social influence and cognitive processes [7]. To this end, the model incorporates constructs such as subjective norm, image, job relevance, output quality, result demonstrability, experience, and voluntariness. Three years later, the unified theory of acceptance and use of technology come to the fore [8]. This theory seeks to predict the intention to use through the variable performance expectancy, effort expectancy, and social influence, which are defined in a way very similar to perceived usefulness, perceived ease of use, and subjective norm, respectively. This set of variables adds up to facilitating conditions, which have a direct effect on usage behavior, and is defined as the extent to which the individual believes that certain organizational and technical infrastructures exist to support the use of a system [8]. Two new variables incorporated into the model correspond to gender and age, which are moderating variables, as well as experience and voluntariness. The

UTAUT2 emerged more recently, as an extension of the UTAUT and to study the acceptance and use of technologies in a consumption context [4]. This model incorporates three new variables, namely, hedonic motivation, price value, and habit.

As for social networks, several authors attempt to explain the use of online social networks (OSNs). According to Schneider et al. [9], users commonly spend more than half an hour interacting with OSNs, and the byte contributions per OSN session are relatively small. From this result, we could assume that most users are consumers and not content creators. In the case of Facebook, Ellison et al. [10] propose that this network might provide greater benefits for users experiencing low self-esteem and low life satisfaction. As for Twitter, Java et al. [11] suggest that people use microblogging to talk about their daily activities and to seek or share information. With respect to Instagram, motives were positively associated with both usage and self-presentation [12]. People use social networks such as Facebook, Twitter, and Instagram for the sole purpose of entertainment and maintaining contacts with their friends' list [13]. As may be seen, the motivations to use social networks are varied. According to Brandtzæg and Heim [14], people use social networks to get in contact with new people, to keep in touch with their friends, and general socializing, and this could be closely related to the variable social influence proposed as a latent exogenous variable in the UTAUT2 [4]. Xu et al. [15] also suggested that user utilitarian gratifications of immediate access and coordination; hedonic gratifications of affection and leisure—which could be related to perceived usefulness and perceived ease of use, respectively; and website social presence were three positive predictors of social network site usage.

Regarding WhatsApp, there are specific motivators linked to cost, sense of community, and immediacy [16], as well as to unlocking new opportunities for intimate communication [17]; addictive behaviors have even been detected toward the application [18]. A number of studies about the use of this innovative technology have been conducted [19], which have detected a series of factors that positively or negatively influence the use of WhatsApp, such as the importance of family groups [20], the use of status within the application [21], interactions with the education field [22, 23], and concerns about privacy [24], among others. This study intends to analyze WhatsApp consumer behavior from the perspective of the variables that influence the intention to use this technology and to determine what these variables are and how they articulate to affect the intention to use WhatsApp, using the variables proposed in the UTAUT2 model [4].

2.2 Methodology

The proposed model considers the following latent exogenous variables that explain the intention to use WhatsApp. The model proposes that the following four variables positively influence the latent endogenous variable behavior.

H1: Hedonic motivation is defined as the pleasure individuals feel when they behave in a certain way or perform a specific activity [25].

H2: Performance expectancy is the extent to which using a technology will provide benefits to consumers in performing certain activities [4].

H3: Effort expectancy is the degree of ease associated with the consumers' use of technology [4].

H4: Social influence is the extent to which consumers perceive that importantly others believe that they should use a particular technology [4]. This social influence or subjective norm is closely related to the intention to use a social network [26–28].

Behavioral intention is defined as the set of motivational factors that indicate how willing people are to try or how much effort people intend to put forth to develop a particular behavior [29].

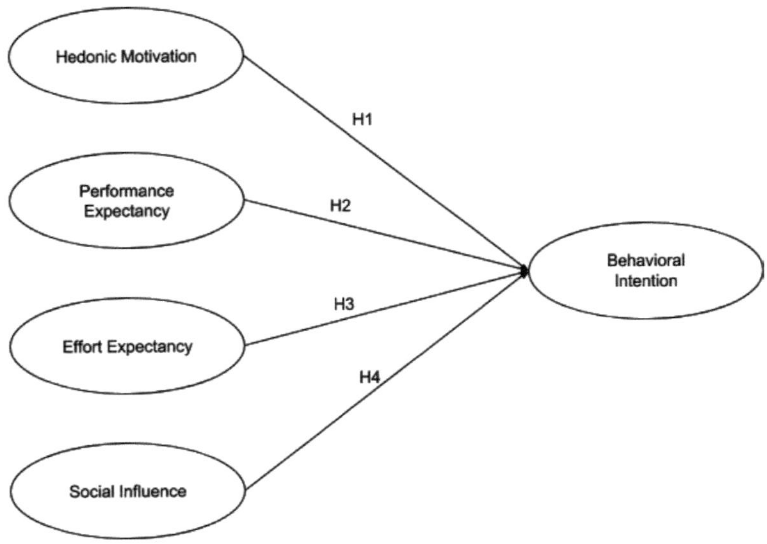

Figure 1.
Proposed model.

The structural model with the latent variables and their proposed relationships is shown in **Figure 1**.

In relation to the latent variables included in the structural model, **Table 1** shows the observable variables measured in the questionnaire. It must be noted that these variables were measured through a Likert scale that ranged from 1 to 5, where 1 means "totally disagree" and 5 "totally agree."

The first four variables refer to performance expectancy, while the four next questions refer to effort expectancy. Then, the following three variables refer to hedonic motivation and the next three to social influence. Finally, the last three questions refer to the behavioral intention of using WhatsApp. The questionnaire also contains variables to measure demographic information such as sex, age, and level of education completed, as well as questions to measure behavioral variables such as the number of hours per day spent using WhatsApp and the number of times per day that respondents use this application.

To conduct this study, a questionnaire was applied that contained the observable variables described above, as well as the questions for demographic characterization. The instrument was applied to 579 people through SurveyMonkey. Sampling was non-probabilistic and by convenience and targeted young people who use the Internet and social networks. The survey was sent through these two channels.

Once answers were collected, a univariate analysis was conducted to obtain the respondents' profile. Afterward, the reliability and internal consistency of each proposed construct were assessed by a Cronbach's alpha test. Finally, the structural analysis proposed in **Figure 1** was carried out using the software IBM SPSS Amos, taking care to obtain adequate absolute, incremental, and parsimony adjustments. Once the structural equation model analysis was completed, a cluster segmentation analysis was executed to determine the different profiles of WhatsApp users based on the answers of the attitude variables proposed in the model.

2.3 Results

First, with respect to the descriptive analysis of the questionnaire answers and as mentioned above, 579 questionnaires were filled out. Fifty-seven percent

I find WhatsApp useful in my daily life
Using WhatsApp increases my chances of achieving things that are important to me
Using WhatsApp helps me accomplish things more quickly
Using WhatsApp increases my productivity
Learning how to use WhatsApp is easy for me
My interaction with WhatsApp is clear and understandable
I find WhatsApp easy to use
It is easy for me to become skillful at using WhatsApp
Using WhatsApp is fun
Using WhatsApp is enjoyable
Using WhatsApp is very entertaining
People who are important to me think that I should use WhatsApp
People who influence my behavior think that I should use WhatsApp
People whose opinions that I value prefer that I use WhatsApp
I intend to continue using WhatsApp in the future
I will always try to use WhatsApp in my daily life
I plan to continue to use WhatsApp frequently

Table 1.
Observed variables.

of respondents are women, 60% of the sample are university students, and 25% completed higher education. In terms of age, the sample is concentrated in an age range from 20 to 40 years, with a mean age of 25.6 years.

Regarding the total of respondents, as shown in **Figure 2**, 62.3% express using WhatsApp for leisure, followed by 23.4% that use it for informative purposes.

When comparing the motives to use WhatsApp by sex, the trend remains constant, with 62.4% of men using WhatsApp for leisure, against 57.5% of women. No significant differences are observed by age and educational level.

Regarding frequency of use, most people report using WhatsApp several times per day (89%): 90.4% for women and 87.1% for men. In this same line, with respect to the observable variables of intention to use, 58.4% of men and 63.6% of women declare totally agreeing that they will continue to use WhatsApp in the future (I intend to continue using WhatsApp in the future), 36.4% of men and 40.0% of women totally agree that they use WhatsApp in their daily life (I will always try to use WhatsApp in my daily life), and 48.0% of men and 53.5% of women declare total agreement with using WhatsApp frequently (I plan to continue to use WhatsApp frequently). In sum, for the three observable variables of the factor intention to use, the percentage of women who totally agree is slightly higher than that of men, and therefore, we can assume that women are more likely to keep using WhatsApp in the future. As seen in the first section, women tend to use mobile devices to access online content more than men, and this trend evidently replicates itself in the use of a mobile app like WhatsApp.

Continuing with the analysis, a Cronbach's alpha reliability test is conducted. Results for each of the four factors proposed in the model from **Figure 1** as latent exogenous variables and the latent endogenous variable behavioral intention are shown in **Table 2**.

All five structural variables yielded satisfactory results in terms of construct reliability, with results over 0.700 in all cases.

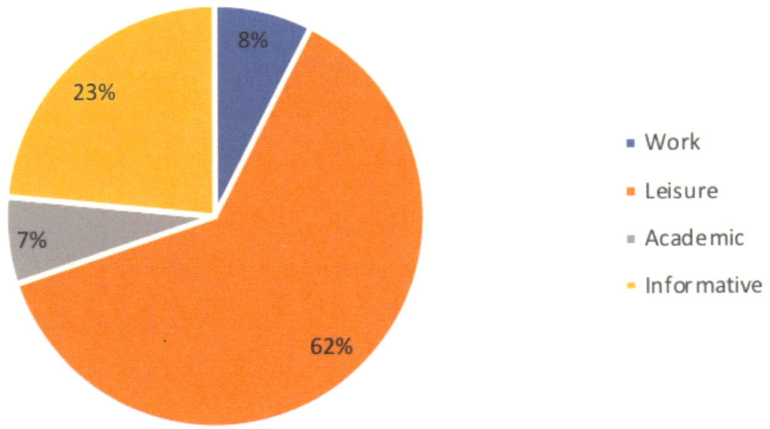

Figure 2.
Main reason why WhatsApp is used.

Performance expectancy	0.736
Effort expectancy	0.801
Social influence	0.867
Hedonic motivation	0.725
Behavioral intention	0.812

Table 2.
Cronbach's α reliability analysis.

Subsequently, the structural model was analyzed using IBM SPSS Amos, obtaining adequate absolute, incremental, and parsimony adjustment. **Figure 3** shows the structural equation modeling, in which all relations proposed are significant (p value < 0.001).

As shown in **Figure 3**, the model reaches R2 = 0.52 to model behavioral intention. In this sense, the most influencing variable is hedonic motivation, with a standardized regression weight of 0.499. Consequently, people use WhatsApp mainly motivated by pleasure, entertainment, and leisure. This is also related to the 62.3% of the sample that stated using WhatsApp for leisure. The other variables that explain the behavioral intention to use this instant messaging application are social influence with a standardized estimate of 0.333, followed by performance expectancy (0.305) and effort expectancy (0.256).

Revising observable variables, it must be noted first that for the factor hedonic motivation, the variable "using WhatsApp is fun" obtains a very high mean of 4.37, while the mode is 5, that is, "totally agree." Indeed, people find that using this app is fun (**Table 3**).

Additionally, it is interesting to observe social influence, in which the variable "people who are important to me think that I should use WhatsApp" obtains a mean of 3.57 and a mode of 3, which implies a certain degree of indifference to social influence. In fact, if the three observable variables of social influence are considered, the mean obtained is 3.75. This might be explained by the fact that individuals do not consider others' opinions to be very relevant when using WhatsApp. This is supported by the standardized regression coefficient 0.333 for this latent exogenous variable in the structural equation model, which albeit statistically significantly does not represent a high impact. A second reading of these results shows that people who are important to the respondent might not approve of the use of

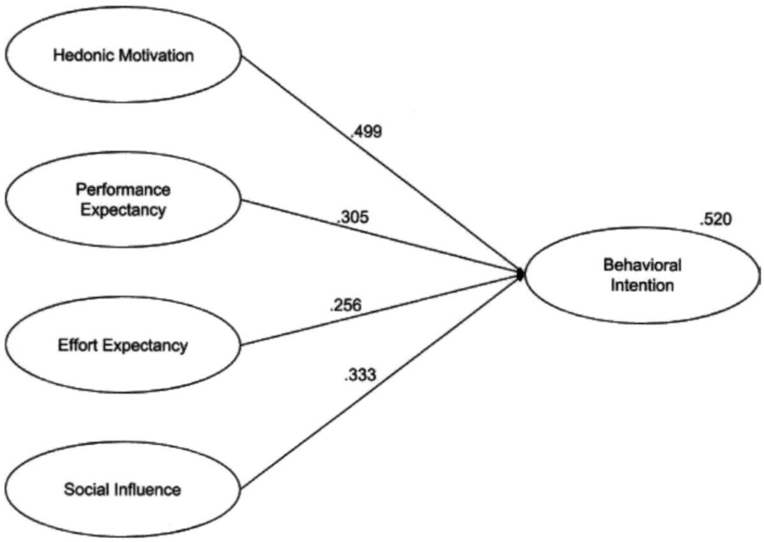

Figure 3.
Result model.

	Mean	Std. deviation
Using WhatsApp is fun	4.37	0.84
Using WhatsApp is enjoyable	4.28	0.89
Using WhatsApp is very entertaining	4.28	0.83

Table 3.
Observable variables of hedonic motivation.

WhatsApp by the respondent, shedding some light on a control problem related to this behavior or perhaps an addiction, as mentioned in the literature review. A third reading leads us to conclude that as WhatsApp is widely used, the opinion of people important to the individual is not absolutely important to him, and what would probably matter would be whether those people use the app. Regardless of the underlying reason, the result is relevant because WhatsApp is an application that allows people to communicate with family and friends, and therefore, a high valuation was expected (between 4 and 5) for the social influence factor (**Table 4**).

Regarding the observable variables of effort expectancy, **Table 5** shows that all have a rather high mean, between 4 and 5, with a standard deviation lower than 0.80 in all cases. In fact, WhatsApp is perceived as easy to use, which, according to the structural equation model, positively contributes to the intention to use the application but to a lesser extent than the other latent variables proposed in the model.

In the case of performance expectancy, it is noteworthy that the observable variable "using WhatsApp increases my productivity" has a high dispersion, with a standard deviation of 1.366 and a mean of 3.07. This casts some doubts on the applicability of the variable to a technology of these characteristics. However, if this variable is removed from the study, the scale of performance expectancy maintains a Cronbach's α of 0.783; therefore, it should not be eliminated. Considering the high dispersion of the answers represented in the standard deviation, we will delve into this point by means of a cluster analysis, since the existence of different segments could help understand this result (**Table 6**).

	Mean	Std. deviation
People who are important to me think that I should use WhatsApp	3.85	1.07
People who influence my behavior think that I should use WhatsApp	3.57	1.09
People whose opinions that I value prefer that I use WhatsApp	3.84	1.08

Table 4.
Observable variables of social influence.

	Mean	Std. deviation
Learning how to use WhatsApp is easy for me	4.66	0.74
My interaction with WhatsApp is clear and understandable	4.54	0.74
I find WhatsApp easy to use	4.68	0.71
It is easy for me to become skillful at using WhatsApp	4.58	0.80

Table 5.
Observable variables of effort expectancy.

	Mean	Std. deviation
I find WhatsApp useful in my daily life	4.47	0.86
Using WhatsApp increases my chances of achieving things that are important to me	3.72	1.21
Using WhatsApp helps me accomplish things more quickly	4.02	1.12
Using WhatsApp increases my productivity	3.07	1.37

Table 6.
Observable variables of performance expectancy.

With the aim of elaborating on the results, a cluster analysis is conducted based on the observable variables of the proposed model. Two segments were found, which do not differ in sex or age but in the usefulness perception of WhatsApp. The values of the four observable variables of performance expectancy are presented in **Table** 7.

A very low valuation by users from Cluster 1 is observed for the variables "using WhatsApp increases my chances of achieving things that are important to me," "using WhatsApp increases my productivity," and "using WhatsApp helps me accomplish things more quickly." This seems to point to the existence of a certain degree of indifference and even disagreement with the contribution of WhatsApp in terms of productivity and utility for the user. In other words, although people from Cluster 1 perceive WhatsApp as useful for their daily routine, this usefulness is not understood as a contribution to their productivity and performance in matters important to them but as a self-referential usefulness. This is completely in agreement with the results, which indicate that people use WhatsApp motivated mainly by leisure, as observed in the first part of the analysis. In addition, individuals from Cluster 1 declare that WhatsApp is a useful app, but it does not help them in their tasks. From this, the following question arises: what is it useful for? Probably this answer has to do with certain degree of causality over other variables, for example, WhatsApp is useful to reach friends or to entertain yourself. But, it is definitely useful in contexts linked to leisure and unrelated to the user's productivity and duties.

It must be also noted that the highest educational level completed by people from Cluster 1 is concentrated in university education and secondary education, while Cluster 2 users have university education and postgraduate studies. This can help explain the differences in performance expectancy, since Cluster 1, represented by university students, does not perceive WhatsApp as a support to its tasks and duties, while Cluster 2, represented by people already in the world of work, does see WhatsApp as a supporting tool for their activities and obligations. This leads us to believe that albeit not the focus of this study, WhatsApp could have a positioning associated with social network and leisure for Cluster 1 and one associated with a messaging app for Cluster 2.

When analyzing the main motive that each cluster has for using WhatsApp, the trend remains constant, with leisure as the dominant motive for Cluster 1 (72.5%) and Cluster 2 (56.4%), although the percentage is slightly lower in the latter, as shown in **Table 8**.

Even when in both cases the major motivation is leisure, it must be noted that differences exist in terms of the distribution of the same. In the case of Cluster 2, the other motives become important, particularly the motive "informative" (21.4%). Moreover, if we had a dichotomy between leisure and non-leisure, in which non-leisure comprises work, study, and information, Cluster 2 would be totally balanced between people who use WhatsApp for leisure and people who use it for other reasons. This obviously helps understand the differences between both segments with respect to the latent exogenous variable "performance expectancy."

Then, an analysis of structural equations is performed seeking to test the proposed model through the samples of the two separate clusters. In this regard, although model fit indices are not optimal, it is necessary to emphasize that the relative weight of each latent exogenous variable on the intention to use WhatsApp responds to the differences shown by both clusters in the previous descriptive analysis. **Figures 4** and **5** show the results of each analysis of structural equations for each cluster.

As shown in **Figure 4**, the most influencing variable is hedonic motivation, with a standardized regression weight of 0.448. Consequently, Cluster 1 uses WhatsApp

	Cluster 1	Cluster 2
I find WhatsApp useful in my daily life	4.01	4.83
Using WhatsApp increases my chances of achieving things that are important to me	2.8	4.21
Using WhatsApp helps me accomplish things more quickly	3.22	4.54
Using WhatsApp increases my productivity	2.3	3.55

Table 7.
Cluster analysis and performance expectancy.

	Cluster 1 (%)	Cluster 2 (%)
Work	7.0	10.7
Leisure	72.5	56.4
Academic	4.2	11.4
Informative	16.2	21.4

Table 8.
Cluster analysis and motivation.

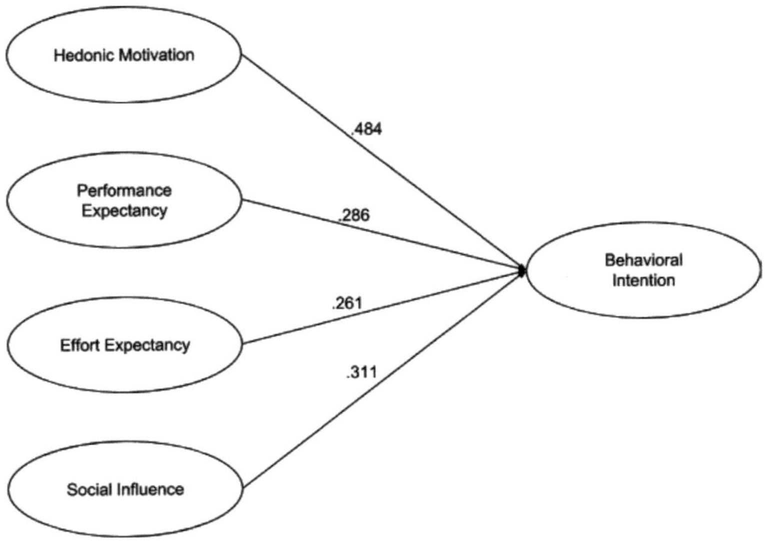

Figure 4.
Cluster 1 result model.

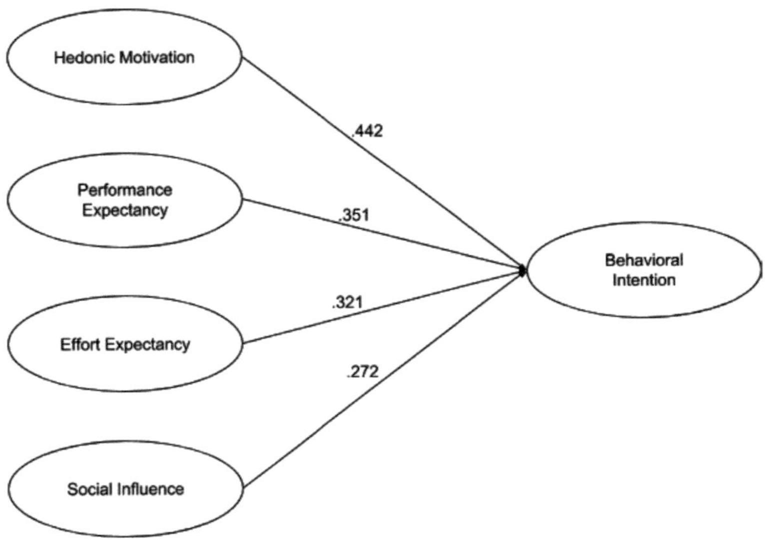

Figure 5.
Cluster 2 result model.

mainly motivated by pleasure, entertainment, and leisure. This is also related to the 72.5% of the cluster that stated using WhatsApp for leisure. The other variables that explain the behavioral intention to use this instant messaging application are social influence with a standardized estimate of 0.311, followed by performance expectancy (0.386) and effort expectancy (0.261). As can be seen, Cluster 1 highlights the importance of hedonic motivation against the other variables with respect to the total sample.

As shown in **Figure 5**, the most influencing variable is hedonic motivation, with a standardized regression weight of 0.442. Consequently, Cluster 2 also uses WhatsApp mainly motivated by pleasure, entertainment, and leisure. This is also related to more than a half of the cluster stated using WhatsApp for leisure. The other variables that explain the behavioral intention to use this instant messaging application are social influence with a standardized estimate of 0.272, followed by performance expectancy (0.351) and effort expectancy (0.321). As can be seen, this cluster also highlights the importance of hedonic motivation against the other variables with respect to the total sample, but there is an increase in the relative weight of the effort expectancy.

To close this point, the results obtained invite us to revise whether the observable variables proposed for performance expectancy can be applied to a technology that is perceived as pertaining to leisure and entertainment.

3. Conclusions

Based on the results of this study, we observe that the most influential variable for the intention to use WhatsApp is hedonic motivation, i.e., people use WhatsApp because it is fun, enjoyable, and very entertaining. This adds up to what is expressed by respondents, who report that their main motivation to use WhatsApp is leisure, which lead us to think that this application is seen more as an entertainment than a communication tool or, in other words, people use this app to communicate with people they are close to and seek entertainment in that interaction, as well as new opportunities for intimate communication [17].

Although all the variables are significant in the proposed model, the low impact of the variable social influence must be highlighted, as this was expected to be much more influential, considering that WhatsApp is an instant messaging application that does not work if people important to the user are not using it. This may indicate that social influence, in the case of an application already in use, translates into whether or not people important to the user's decision-making process use the app and is not related to the opinion these people have regarding the user's conduct.

Furthermore, the variability of the responses in the observable variables of the dimension performance expectancy seems to indicate that WhatsApp may have use drivers that vary among groups of people. To support this hypothesis, the cluster analysis yields two groups of users, whose main difference is related to the valuation of the observable variables of the dimension performance expectancy as well as the main motivation to use this application. As mentioned above, people in general use WhatsApp for leisure and entertainment; however, a great part of Cluster 2 declares that they use the app for motives other than leisure. Consequently, Cluster 1 presents valuations of indifference and disagreement regarding the usefulness of WhatsApp for their activities and duties. Consequently, there are at least two different segments of WhatsApp users motivated by different reasons, even though cross-cutting leisure and entertainment is the main motivation to continue using this technology.

From an AI/ML perspective, this study helps to guide the way in which the software behind WhatsApp should conduct their different learning processes about the user. Indeed, if we consider the results described above where hedonic motivation and social influence are the variables with the greatest influence on behavioral intention, WhatsApp should aim to develop its ML in the sense of generating updates that allow greater fun and entertainment to its users, with virtual reality features, camera filters, new emojis, photo effects and filters, and even games. In summary, WhatsApp could guide their ML to know in a better way how the user enjoys using WhatsApp, making it an increasingly entertaining mobile application.

Likewise, considering the social influence, WhatsApp should guide its AI toward a greater social role as a messaging application, similar to Facebook and other social networks, where the user can connect with new "recommended friends," for example, according to their common interests and according to the number of contacts in common. In summary, the development of AI in WhatsApp could be oriented to a social network role over a simple instant messaging application.

Finally, the present chapter helps to understand what variables are involved in the behavior of users of these applications, information that can be used for the development of AI/ML ability of this application, making it adaptive to the needs of the user that can vary according to the context and the expected benefit, as our cluster analysis shows, ergo, to find ways to present the right service at the right time and with the right quality [30]. As stated before, this study also evidences the existence of consumer clusters in which users satisfy different needs with this mobile application, which indeed represents new opportunities for similar applications that aim to challenge the dominance of WhatsApp on the instant messaging field.

Acknowledgements

WhatsApp, Instagram, and Facebook are registered trademarks, and the author only uses them as a reference in his study due to the high level of use by the world population.

Author details

Cristobal Fernández-Robin[1*], Diego Yáñez[1] and Scott McCoy[2]

1 Federico Santa María Technical University, Valparaíso, Chile

2 Mason School of Business, Williamsburg, VA, USA

*Address all correspondence to: cristobal.fernandez@usm.cl

References

[1] Bock W, Field D, Zwillenberg P, Rogers K: The growth of the global mobile internet economy: The connected world. The Boston Consulting Group [Internet]. 2015. Available from: https://www.bcg.com/publications/2015/technology-industries-growth-global-mobile-internet-economy.aspx [Accessed: August 29, 2018]

[2] Martin B. The Global Mobile Report. comScore [Internet]. 2017. Available from: https://www.comscore.com/Insights/Presentations-and-Whitepapers/2017/The-Global-Mobile-Report [Accessed: August 29, 2018]

[3] Smith C. DMR [Internet]. 2018. Available from: http://expandedramblings.com [Accessed: August 22, 2018]

[4] Venkatesh V, Thong J, Xu X. Consumer acceptance and use of information technology: Extending the unified theory of acceptance and use of technology. MIS Quarterly. 2012;**36**(1):157-178

[5] Fishbein M, Ajzen I. Belief, Attitude, Intention, and Behavior: An Introduction to Theory and Research. 4th ed. Vol. 578. Reading, MA: Addison-Wesley; 1980

[6] Davis F. Perceived usefulness, perceived ease of use, and user acceptance of information technology. MIS Quarterly. 1989;**13**(3):319-340

[7] Venkatesh V, Davis F. A theoretical extension of the technology acceptance model: Four longitudinal field studies. Management Science. 2000;**46**(2):186-204

[8] Venkatesh V, Morris M, Davis G, Davis F. User acceptance of information technology: Toward a unified view. MIS Quarterly. 2003;**27**(3):425-478. DOI: 10.2307/30036540

[9] Schneider F, Feldmann A, Krishnamurthy B, Willinger W. Understanding online social network usage from a network perspective. In: Proceedings of the 9th ACM SIGCOMM Conference on Internet Measurement; November 2009; Chicago, Illinois, USA. pp. 35-48

[10] Ellison N, Steinfield C, Lampe C. The benefits of facebook "friends": Social capital and college students' use of online social network sites. Journal of Computer-Mediated Communication. 2007;**12**(4):1143-1168. DOI: 10.1111/j.1083-6101.2007.00367.x

[11] Java A, Song X, Finin T, Tseng B. Why we twitter: Understanding microblogging usage and communities. In: Proceedings of the 9th WebKDD and 1st SNA-KDD 2007 Workshop on Web Mining and Social Network Analysis; August 2007; San Jose, California: ACM. pp. 56-65

[12] Cheung T. A study on motives, usage, self-presentation and number of followers on Instagram [thesis]. Hong Kong: City University of Hong Kong; 2014

[13] Narula S, Jindal N. Use of social network sites by AUMP students: A comparative study on Facebook, Twitter and Instagram usage. Journal of Advanced Research. 2015;**2**(2):20-24

[14] Brandtzæg P, Heim J. Why people use social networking sites. Online Communities and Social Computing. 2009;**5621**:143-152. DOI: 10.1007/978-3-642-02774-1_16

[15] Xu C, Ryan S, Prybutok V, Wen C. It is not for fun: An examination of social network site usage. Information and Management. 2012;**49**(5):210-217. DOI: 10.1016/j.im.2012.05.001

[16] Church K, de Oliveira R. What's up with WhatsApp?: Comparing mobile

instant messaging behaviors with traditional SMS. In: Proceedings of the 15th International Conference on Human-Computer Interaction with Mobile Devices and Services; August 2013; Munich, Germany. pp. 352-361

[17] Karapanos E, Teixeira P, Gouveia R. Need fulfillment and experiences on social media: A case on Facebook and WhatsApp. Computers in Human Behavior. 2016;**55**:888-897. DOI: 10.1016/j.chb.2015.10.015

[18] Sultan A. Addiction to mobile text messaging applications is nothing to "lol" about. The Social Science Journal. 2014;**51**(1):57-69. DOI: 10.1016/j.soscij.2013.09.003

[19] Pielot M, de Oliveira R, Kwak H, Oliver N. Didn't you see my message?: Predicting attentiveness to mobile instant messages. In: Proceedings of the 32nd Annual ACM Conference on Human Factors in Computing Systems; May 2014; Toronto, Ontario, Canada. pp. 3319-3328

[20] Aharony N, Gazit T. The importance of the WhatsApp family group: An exploratory analysis. Aslib Journal of Information Management. 2016;**68**(2):174-192. DOI: 10.1108/AJIM-09-2015-0142

[21] Sánchez-Moya A, Cruz-Moya O. "Hey there! I am using WhatsApp": A preliminary study of recurrent discursive realisations in a corpus of WhatsApp statuses. Procedia - Social and Behavioral Sciences. 2015;**212**:52-60. DOI: 10.1016/j.sbspro.2015.11.298

[22] Bouhnik D, Deshen M. WhatsApp goes to school: Mobile instant messaging between teachers and students. Journal of Information Technology Education Research. 2014;**13**:217-231

[23] So S. Mobile instant messaging support for teaching and learning in higher education. The Internet and Higher Education. 2016;**31**:32-42. DOI: 10.1016/j.iheduc.2016.06.001

[24] Rashidi Y, Vanie, K, Camp L. Understanding Saudis' privacy concerns when using WhatsApp. In: Proceedings of the Workshop on Usable Security (USEC'16); February 2016; San Diego, California, USA. pp. 1-8

[25] Moon J, Kim Y. Extending the TAM for a world-wide-web context. Information and Management. 2001;**38**(4):217-230. DOI: 10.1016/S0378-7206(00)00061-6

[26] Chen Y. See you on Facebook: Exploring influences on Facebook continuous usage. Behaviour & Information Technology. 2014;**33**(11):1208-1218. DOI: 10.1080/0144929X.2013.826737

[27] Li D. Online social network acceptance: A social perspective. Internet Research. 2011;**21**(5):562-580. DOI: 10.1108/10662241111176371

[28] Pelling E, White K. The theory of planned behavior applied to young people's use of social networking web sites. CyberPsycholy & Behaviour. 2009;**12**(6):755-759. DOI: 10.1089/cpb.2009.0109

[29] Ajzen I. The theory of planned behavior. Organizational Behavior and Human Decision Processes. 1991;**50**(2):179-211. DOI: 10.1016/0749-5978(91)90020-T

[30] Harkut, D. (2011). e-CRM–Data Modeling Using Adaptive Neuro Fuzzy model. International Journal of Business and Information Technology. **1**(2): 130-136

Chapter 3

Information and Communication Systems Including Artificial Intelligence and Big Data as Objects of International Legal Protection

Valentina Petrovna Talimonchik

Abstract

The objective of this study is identifying prospective for international legal protection of information and communication systems including artificial intelligence on the universal and regional levels, and analysis of legal instruments for protection of artificial intelligence and Big Data in the context of regulation of relations in the global information society. A complex of general scientific and philosophical methods, including the logical, comparative-legal, formal-legal, systemic-structural, and problematic-theoretical methods, as well as methods of analysis and synthesis, generalization and description were used in the research. It was found that the existing international agreements in the field of intellectual property protection take no account of the particular features of protection of complex objects. Complex objects comprise information and communication systems including artificial intelligence and Big Data. There is an objective necessity to establish a legal regime for complex objects on the universal level. The findings can be used in activities of international organizations in execution of their functions of unification and harmonization of the international information law.

Keywords: information and communication systems, international legal protection, artificial intelligence, big data, databases, computer programs

1. Introduction

The international protection of intellectual property began to take form in the late nineteenth century. Characteristically, that was the time when the stable basis of international cooperation in the field of intellectual property was established. With regard to copyright, the Berne Convention for the Protection of Literary and Artistic Works was adopted in 1886, and protection of patent rights was introduced by the Paris Convention for the Protection of Industrial Property in 1883.

The development of intellectual property protection on the universal level can be described as conservative. With new technologies emerging, the existing international treaties were revised only slightly to adapt to the regulation of new technologies. For example, when the Berne Convention was revised in 1908 in

Berlin, the range of objects of protection was extended to works of choreography, entertainments in dumb show, cinematography, architecture, and photography.

Until the middle of the twentieth century, the influence of scientific and technical progress on the development of copyright and patent law was very insignificant. The advent of radio and television caused significant change in the system of related rights. There appeared new objects of related rights, namely phonograms and broadcasts.

In the twentieth century, scientific and technical progress caused radical changes in the contemporary world. The system of social relations has changed. The development of information and communication technologies (ICTs) has affected all the aspects of social life including the economy, politics, welfare sphere, and culture.

Modern information technologies cannot develop within the borders of a particular state. They are transborder by their nature.

By the present time, the information society theory has been reflected in a number of international documents. These include the Okinawa Charter on Global Information Society of July 22, 2000, the Declaration of Principles "Building the Information Society: A Global Challenge in the New Millennium", and the Plan of Action of the World Summit on the Information Society of December 12, 2003.

There is no consensus in the doctrine about the moment when the theory of an informational society appeared. Matterlart [1] has identified early beginnings of the information society theory. His research of information society theories begins from Leibniz (1646–1716) who was the first to put the set of numbers in order and give it a strict hierarchy. He is also the author of the idea of a universal mathematical language, the so-called binary number system, which was later used in cybernetics.

Without dismissing the achievements of the thinkers of the seventeenth to nineteenth centuries, we must note that the first sociological studies of the information society were made in the 1960s.

The task of systematization of ideas about the information society is complicated by the fact that researchers have often made assumptions about ideal information society and social forecasts, the reliability of which is too early to discuss.

For demonstrating the diversity of information society theories, we will use the classification by Webster [2]. He identified five groups of information society theories, namely technological, economic, occupational, spatial, and cultural.

The diversity of information society theories is explained by the fact that there are many factors and phenomena interacting in the information society.

In our view, contemporary relations in creation, distribution, receiving, storage, transmission, and destruction of information are characterized by a broad range of subjects. We agree with Masuda who claims that "the most advanced stage of the information society will be the high mass knowledge creation society, in which computerization will make it possible for each person to create knowledge and to go on to self-fulfillment" [3]. Individuals and associations of individuals, such as legal entities, social associations, etc. are increasingly becoming subjects of information relations. This is due to the fact that ICT allows direct communication between people without regard to state borders. Thus, it becomes possible for nonstate subjects to participate in information relations, which does not exclude the participation of states in such relations.

In the information society, the protection of intellectual property is a key factor for its development.

The Okinawa Charter on Global Information Society stated that protecting the intellectual property rights for information technology is important for promoting IT-related innovations, promoting competition, and widespread introduction of new technologies. The Charter welcomed the cooperation within intellectual property authorities and further discussion of experts in this area. It should be noted that the Charter provided protection of intellectual property for information technologies, an object not covered by the 1886 Berne Convention for the Protection of Literary and Artistic Works and the 1883 Paris Convention for the Protection of Industrial Property.

At present, the development of relations in the global information society is facing the problem of insufficient legal protection of scientific and technical achievements.

The problems of intellectual property protection are considered in fundamental studies on information technology law including Bainbridge [4], Campbell and Ban [5], Rowland and Macdonald [6], Lloyd [7], and Murray [8].

At the same time, there are no monographic researches on problems of international legal protection of information systems as complex objects.

2. Concept headings

The objective of the research is identifying prospective for international legal protection of information and communication systems including artificial intelligence on the universal and regional levels, and analysis of legal instruments for protection of artificial intelligence and Big Data in the context of regulation of relations in the global information society. In order to achieve the objectives of the research, it is necessary, first of all, to analyze the existing systems for protection of computer programs and databases.

In the legal doctrine, publications on the use of artificial intelligence in law enforcement and the legal profession first appeared in the 1980s [9, 10].

At present, there are hundreds of publications on the matter of legal problems associated with artificial intelligence, and discussions concerning issues of legal capacity and liability relating to problems of the theory of law, as well as research of branches of national law.

The contribution of international law experts in the considered problems is not as significant. In particular, there is a very in-depth study on international humanitarian law [11]. The doctrine has analyzed matters of the Big Data impact on human rights [12] and the connection between Big Data and progressive development of international law [13].

The questions that must be answered in this study are as follows. What legal protection on the universal level must be provided to information and communication systems? What are information and communication systems as objects of international legal regulation?

The object closest to artificial intelligence, which is protected on the universal level, is computer programs.

The legal protection of computer programs appeared before the electronic communications technology and has developed step by step. In the early 1960s, the legal protection of software was provided on the national level. Because computer programs were regarded as unique, since the production and use of computers were not yet a mass phenomenon, it was the patent protection of software that was considered the basic method at the first stage of development of the legal regulation of software and database protection. The patent protection of software had been used in the USA since the 1960s. Initially, the US Patent and Trademark Office refused to patent computer programs, regarding them as mental objects. However, in 1968, the Court of Appeals made conclusions on the patentability of algorithms, computational techniques, and code building methods in several judgments.

In the 1960s and 1970s, the patent protection of software was completely adequate to the achieved level of technical development and applied in all countries with a sufficiently high level of computer technology development. In particular, in Germany, the patent protection of software appeared in 1973 after a number of relevant judgments by the Federal Patent Court.

Since the second half of the 1970s, the next stage of development of the legal protection of software began. The approach to the content of the legal protection of software changed significantly. Because computer technologies gradually became more widespread, and computers penetrated all the areas of social life, some computer programs no longer met the requirements of novelty. Change in the approach to the legal protection of software occurred on the universal level. In 1978, the Advisory Group of Non-Governmental Experts of the International Bureau of WIPO developed the Model Provisions on the Protection of Computer Software.

The Advisory Group of Non-Governmental Experts of the International Bureau of WIPO began the development of the Model Provisions on the Protection of Computer Software in 1971 when patent protection was applied widely on the national level. However, the solution that was later proposed by WIPO was significantly different from the existing practice in particular states. The experts remarked that the Model Provisions were not proposed to states as a single model act. The principles of the Model Provisions could be embodied in parts in copyright and patent law and in competition law.

However, the provision that the principles of the Model Provisions could be embodied in various legal institutions did not imply the possibility of integral protection of software. From the contents of Sections 3 and 4 of the Model Provisions, it followed that software must be protected by copyright law of the relevant state. In particular, Section 3 of the Model Provisions stipulated that software must be original in the meaning of copyright of the relevant state and contained a general originality requirement, namely that software must be a result of its creator's own intellectual efforts. According to Section 4, it was the form and not the idea of software that must be protected.

It is characteristic that in 1978, Professor Herbert Simon won the Nobel Premium in Economics for his pioneering research in the decision-making process within economic organizations, which contains the theory of bounded rationality, a key concept for artificial intelligence.

This overview of history does not seem out of place in view of the practice of national courts on the patentability of artificial intelligence, which was summarized by Hashiguchi [14].

In the USA, an example of recognition of the patentability of a method for automatic animation of synchronization of the lips and facial expression in computer graphics is the case of McRO. Inc. v. Bandai Namco Games America Inc. The federal court found that this method is patentable because it does not lead to an abstract idea. The court took account of the specifics of the automatic method, which covered individual operations with specific characteristics. The method comprising individual operations was designed for the transfer of information in a specific format, which was used for creating characters. Features of the industrial applicability of this invention were also taken into account. Firstly, it is not just a methodology as such that is used. Secondly, the invention could not be used without using a computer technology. Overall, the court concluded that processes which automate the tasks performed by people are patentable.

The US courts are guided primarily by the criterion of the utility of the invention with elements of artificial intelligence.

Boards of Appeal of the European Patent Office are bound by the provisions of Article 52 of the European Patent Convention of 1973. Discoveries, scientific theories and mathematical methods, esthetic creations, schemes, rules and methods for performing mental acts, playing games or doing business, and programs for computers and presentations of information are not considered inventions. Therefore, a method or a program may not be patented, but technical devices that use them may. The Board of Appeal recognized a server for automatic document collection and a device for creating three-dimensional models as patentable.

Given the experience of the legal protection of computer software, it is unlikely that the idea of patentability of inventions with elements of artificial intelligence will be supported on the universal level.

The object closest to Big Data, which is protected on the universal level, is databases.

The development of intellectual property protection on the universal level can be described as conservative. With new technologies emerging, the existing international agreements were revised only slightly to adapt to the regulation of new technologies.

The need for compliance of the legal means for protection with the features of protected objects was manifested more clearly when the Directive 96/9/EC of the European Parliament and Council on the legal protection of databases of March 11, 1996, was adopted. This Directive provided a sui generis right. A prerequisite for this right is the "substantial investment", which is required for creating the objects of the new right. The sui generis right to databases is protected for 15 years and includes exclusive control of the database creator over the recovery and reuse of its contents.

In the legal doctrine, the appearance of the sui generis right is associated with the problem of the legal protection of nonoriginal works. According to Jehoram, copyright is not an appropriate way to protect databases. This is why the Directive on Databases provides sui generis protection for those databases which are not original. [15].

Without consideration of the EU experience, in the WIPO Copyright Treaty of December 20, 1996, it is stated that computer programs and databases are protected by copyright. According to Article 1 of this Treaty, it is a special agreement within the meaning of Article 20 of the Berne Convention for the Protection of Literary and Artistic Works. Article 4 of the Agreement stipulates that computer programs are protected as literary works within the meaning of Article 2 of the Berne Convention. Such protection applies to computer programs, whatever may be the mode or form of their expression. Article 5 of the Treaty stipulates that databases are protected as such if they contain elements of intellectual creativity. The protection provided cannot pretend that the data and materials in the database are relevant to copyright. Provisions on the legal protection of computer programs and databases are contained in Articles 1–7 of the Treaty. Matters of legal protection are regulated in the Treaty in the most general form, for which reason the content of the Treaty is not satisfactory enough for the necessities of the regulation of the protection of software and databases on the universal level.

At the same time, national laws (e.g., in France, Switzerland, and Germany) provide copyright protection for databases.

Stipulation of the protection of computer programs and databases in the laws of a number of states in a form not specific enough has led to a number of problems with the implementation of such legal provisions. There is no doubt that the terms "publication" and "copying" as applied to computer programs and databases have special features that distinguish them from traditional copyright objects. If there are no definitions of such terms in the law, their meaning can only be clarified in view of the existing practice of judicial and administrative authorities of particular states.

In regard of law enforcement difficulties, of significant interest is the practice of the US Copyright Office, an analysis of which was made by their officer Oler [16]. The Copyright Office registered databases as "books" in class A, but the originality requirements for registration were not as strict. The Copyright Office regarded publication as reproduction of the program in a form that is perceivable or accessible for the human eyes. The date of the first publication was traditionally understood as the date when the program was sold or offered for sale to consumers. As for copying, copies of the program could be typewritten or contained on floppy disks or in interfaces. The main criterion for copying is creation of copies in a language that can be understood by humans.

At present, one should take account of the fact that functions of programs and databases have changed in the 1980s–1990s. Computer programs and databases are becoming all the more important not just as individual technical phenomena but as crucial components of computer networks, which are a qualitatively new technical phenomenon. Therefore, the legal provisions on the protection of software and databases in the laws of various countries should be specific and, to the extent possible, similar.

The WIPO Copyright Treaty of 1996 and the TRIPS Agreement contain quite concise regulations in respect of computer programs. For example, Article 4 of the WIPO Treaty and Article 10 of TRIPS stipulate that computer programs are protected as literary works in the meaning of the Berne Convention.

At the same time, the development of the provisions of the Berne Convention in these instruments is different. The special features of computer programs are taken into account only in Article 11 of the TRIPS Agreement. In relation to, at least, computer programs, a Party should grant authors and their assignees the right to authorize or prohibit public commercial rental of originals or copies of their copyrighted works. This obligation does not apply to commercial rental when the program itself is not the main object of rental.

The WIPO Treaty of 1996 regulates the protection of computer programs in greater detail. The right of rental is stipulated by Article 7 of the Treaty. However, in order to understand the scope of the legal protection of computer programs, one should take account of the Agreed Statements concerning the WIPO Copyright Treaty related to the additional means of interpretation of this Treaty (Article 32 of the Vienna Convention on the Law of International Treaties of 1969).

Firstly, the right of reproduction, which was provided for Article 9 of the Berne Convention, and the exceptions from this right allowed by this article, are applied in the digital environment. It is understood that the storage of works in digital form in an electronic medium is a reproduction in the sense of Article 9 of the Bern Convention. At the same time, states may establish exceptions to the right of reproduction in certain special cases, provided that such reproduction does not prejudice the normal use of the work and does not unreasonably harm the author's legitimate interests. In addition, the provisions of the 1996 WIPO Copyright Treaty allow states to transfer and appropriately extend to the digital environment limitations and exceptions that are considered acceptable under the Berne Convention. Similarly, the provisions of the Berne Convention should be understood as allowing states to define new exceptions and limitations that are suitable in the digital computer network environment.

Secondly, it should be noted that copyright protection extends to expressions and not to ideas, procedures, methods of operation, or mathematical concepts as such. As a result, the form of expression of the program is protected.

Thirdly, it is understood that the reference to "infringement of any right covered by this Treaty or the Berne Convention" includes both exclusive rights and rights of remuneration.

Therefore, systemic interpretation of the 1996 WIPO Treaty has identified a number of harmonization provisions allowing states to provide conditions for protection of computer programs, the scope of the author's rights, and exceptions from legal protection in their national laws.

It should be noted that the approach applied in these agreements takes no account of the features of computer programs as a result of scientific and technical activity. More acceptable is the EU approach where there is a more detailed regulation for computer programs.

In particular, in the Council Directive 91/250/EEC of May 14, 1991 on the legal protection of computer programs, the rights of the author are regulated in relation to the features of computer programs. These include persistent or temporary reproduction of a computer program by any means and in any form, including downloading, transmitting, or accumulating a program and any other action and any form of public distribution, including rental of the original computer program or its copies.

The special features of the object of protection also show in the exceptions made by the Directive. Permission from the copyright holder to actions that are necessary for the use of a computer program by the legal acquirer in accordance with its intentions, including the correction of errors, is not required. Production of an outdated copy by a person authorized to use a computer program may not be prohibited by a contract if it is necessary for such use.

The person who has the right to use a copy of a computer program is given the right to view, study, or check the work of the program without the permission of right holder in order to determine the ideas and principles that underlie any element of the program.

The nature of the abovementioned exceptions is such that they aim to enable normal use of the program and make the use of the program convenient for the user. This way, a balance of public and private interests is achieved with regard to the use of protected objects.

It can be concluded from the provisions of the Directive that the provisions on the protection of computer programs are special in the framework of copyright. However, this specificity is not taken into account in regulation on the universal level.

3. Results

It is obvious that artificial intelligence cannot be regarded as an "ordinary" computer program in the meaning of the abovementioned international legal acts. According to TRIPS, computer programs, whether in source or object code, shall be protected. According to the 1991 Directive, the legal protection applies to computer programs and their preparatory design material. This regulation is substantially different from the regulation in the Model Provisions on the Protection of Computer Software developed by the WIPO experts. According to the Model Provisions, protection should apply not just to the abovementioned objects but also to the program use manuals, which are not protected objects in Europe.

It is easy to notice that artificial intelligence is a more complex object by its structure. It is an information and communication system capable of synthesizing creative activity in the literary, artistic, and industrial areas.

Big data is an object close to artificial intelligence if one considers the practice of national courts on the patentability of artificial intelligence, which was summarized by Hashiguchi [14].

In the LLC v. Microsoft Corporation case, the invention of self-assembled databases was considered patentable. Usually, the database structure is determined by computer programs. For the LLC database, no program was needed, as the database configured itself. The District Court for the Central District of California resolved that the object is unpatentable and that it is an abstract idea. However, the federal court drew attention to the fact that the invention improves the computer capacities in a certain way and that it is a particular technical solution of a problem in the field of software. The significant contribution of the invention to the development of computer technology was noted.

Therefore, in the terms of technology there is a "convergence" of artificial intelligence and Big Data.

It is obvious that Big Data should not be regarded as an ordinary database. It is easy to notice that Big Data is a more complex object by structure. It is an information and communication system capable of collecting and processing information and providing access to it, in particular, with engagement of artificial intelligence.

As concerns Article 2 of the Berne Convention, one can conclude that the Berne Convention does not cover complex objects of copyright. These cannot include lectures, addresses, sermons, books, pamphlets, photographic works, works of drawing, painting, architecture, sculpture, engraving and lithography, works of applied art, illustrations, maps, plans, sketches, and three-dimensional works relative to geography, topography, architecture, or science. Dramatic and dramatico-musical works, choreographic works, and entertainments in dumb show are components of a theater performance, which is a more complex object. Basically, the only complex object that is regulated by the Berne Convention is cinematographic works to which are assimilated works expressed by a process analogous to cinematography, primarily through harmonization provisions. However, the regulation of cinematographic works in the Berne Convention cannot be considered sufficient. The legal provisions are too laconic. Without prejudice to the copyright of any work that could be redone or reproduced, the cinematographic work is protected as the original work. The copyright holder of a cinematographic work has the same rights as the author of the original work. The Convention does not determine the circle of copyright holders for cinematographic works. However, in the countries of the Union, the legislation of which includes to copyright holders of a cinematographic work authors who contributed to its creation, these authors have no right to oppose the reproduction, distribution, public presentation and performance, communication to the public by wire, broadcast, or any other communication to the public, as well as captioning and duplication of the text. States implement this provision on the terms and conditions stated in the Berne Convention.

As a result, it becomes necessary to establish the legal regime for complex objects in additional act for the Berne Convention. This applies not just to artificial intelligence and Big Data but also to other results of the infocommunication revolution including websites, computer models, television format, and audiovisual format.

WIPO realizes the importance of the problem of artificial intelligence. In the address of the General Director of WIPO at the session of the Assembly of the Member States of WIPO (October 2–11, 2017), there is the following statement that should be commented: "A final area that I shall mention, where I believe that the Organization should commence to engage, although perhaps with baby steps, is the rapidly developing area of big data, the Internet of Things and artificial intelligence. The area has enormous implications and a multiplicity of dimensions, many of which lie well beyond the focus of intellectual property, and considerable care will need to be exercised to ensure that we do not stray from the mandate of the Organization. One focus of attention could be the increasing use of artificial intelligence and big data in IP administration. We have developed several applications—in translation, classification, and image-searching—and a number of IP Offices are likewise working on different applications. In order to keep IP administration abreast of the latest technological developments, it would be useful if we develop mechanisms for sharing information about our respective work, as well as for taking advantage of each other's work and avoiding duplication."

As we see, WIPO is just beginning to understand the new phenomena, and no steps are made concerning their regulation. The issues discussed by the Standing Committee on Copyright Law and Related Rights (SCCR) are copyright limitations and exceptions for educational institutions, libraries, and archives, and the draft WIPO Treaty to Protection Broadcasting Organizations. Matters related to new technologies are far away from the SCCR's agenda.

The Special Union for the International Patent Classification intends to use the opportunities of artificial intelligence in their activities. Its Committee of Experts examines applications of the EPO/USA and Japan on the review of the classification in the NET area; for CPC or the File Index (FI), it is planned to include new NET areas because this measure would lead to maximum benefit for the IPC. However, it should be noted that the IPC may not oblige states to provide patent protection to inventions containing artificial intelligence. States determine the legal value of the IPC for their legal systems independently. Therefore, it is too early to speak about the establishment of patent protection for artificial intelligence on the universal level.

However, the problem cannot be solved with efforts of WIPO alone. As a complex object, Big Data also requires other regimes of legal protection including protection of the privacy of individuals and legal entities and protection of trade, medical, and other protected secrets.

The privacy protection system has already been developed on the universal level. Currently, the protection of privacy has a treaty origin. Provisions for protection of privacy are stipulated in Article 17 of the 1966 International Covenant on Civil and Political Rights, Article 8 of the 1950 European Convention for the Protection of Human Rights and Fundamental Freedoms, and Article 11 of the 1969 American Convention on Human Rights.

Article 17 of the 1966 International Covenant on Civil and Political Rights stipulates that no one may be subjected to unlawful interference with his private and family life, unlawful attacks on the inviolability of his home or the secrecy of his correspondence, or unlawful attacks on his honor and reputation. Everyone has the right to the protection of the law against such interference or such encroachment. Similar provisions are stipulated by regional international treaties.

Article 27 of the Customs Code of the Eurasian Economic Union of 2017 stipulates that information from preliminary decisions on classification of goods, excluding the information that constitutes state, trade, banking, or other secret protected by law or other confidential information, which relates to the person concerned, shall be published on the official website of the Union. Article 38 of the above-mentioned document contains a rule that in the course of consultations, customs authorities and applicants may exchange information on the condition of compliance with the trade secret laws of the member states. Trade secrets can be a subject of interstate information exchange between customs authorities. During customs inspections, officials of the customs authority are entitled to request documents and information that are necessary for the customs inspection including ones that constitute trade, banking, tax, or other secrets protected by law from state bodies of the member states and receive the same from them in accordance with the laws of the member states. State bodies of the member states shall on request of the customs authority provide them with documents and information that they have with regard to registration of organizations and individual entrepreneurs, payment and accrual of taxes, accounting and reporting data or/and documents, and other documents and information that are necessary for customs inspections including ones that constitute trade, banking, tax, or other secrets protected by law, in accordance with the laws of the member states on protection of the state, trade, banking, tax, and other secrets protected by law. Experts who are engaged from other state authorities of member states must not disclose information that constitute trade, banking, tax, or other secrets protected by law or confidential information related to participants of foreign economic and other activities in the customs field. The same obligation has been imposed on customs authorities, their officials, customs representatives, and customs carriers.

Issues of trade secret are regulated by bilateral international treaties on cooperation in the field of science, technology, and innovations, on cooperation in the field of exploration and use of outer space for peaceful purposes, on cooperation and mutual administrative assistance in customs matters, and on mutual protection of rights to intellectual property that are used and generated in the course of bilateral cooperation in the field of military technology.

On the universal scale, trade secrets are protected by TRIPS. Protection of undisclosed information is provided in the course of ensuring protection against unfair competition as provided in Article 10bis of the Paris Convention (1967). States are also expressly obliged to protect undisclosed information obtained by them as a condition of approving the marketing of pharmaceutical or agricultural products which utilize new chemical entities.

It should be noted that part 2 of this Article of TRIPS entitles the holders of undisclosed information to determine its regulation. Individuals and legal entities are given the opportunity to prevent information under their control, without their consent, being disclosed, obtained or used by other persons in a manner contrary to honest commercial practice, if such information:

- is secret in the sense that it as a whole or in a certain configuration and selection of its components is not well known and easily accessible;

- has commercial value because it is secret; and

- is subject to appropriate measures in these circumstances, aimed at preserving its secrecy, on the part of the person legally controlling this information.

However, Article 39 of TRIPS is not adapted well to tort relations in the field of information. A number of foreign states know the practice of special conflict of law regulation of defamation and privacy. Special conflict of law provisions for defamation and privacy exist in the UK, USA, Switzerland, Japan, China, and Turkey. We could not find any special conflict of law regulation of issues of trade and other secrets. Most often, the holder of the secret is interested in preventing the spread of information and prohibiting its use in the offender's business, which makes special conflict of law regulation necessary.

4. Discussion

The issue of the implementation of privacy protection in the use of Big Data has already been considered in fundamental research in information technology. Rowland et al. [17] have addressed EU acts when considering privacy problems, regarding problems of their application in the use of Big Data. However, the problems of the use of regional experience on the universal level were not covered by this study.

An identical approach to definition of personal data is characteristic of the OECD Guidelines governing the Protection of Privacy and Transborder Flows of Personal Data of September 23, 1980, and the 1981 Convention for the Protection of Individuals with regard to the Automatic Processing of Personal Data. In these documents, personal data are defined as any information related to an identified or identifiable individual. Therefore, protected data include any information about an individual that can be identified. Such a broad range of protected information makes it possible to protect personal data in the situation of changing technologies that are used to collect and process data. In particular, protected data include PIN codes, logins, passwords, etc.

Certain provisions are applied only to individuals, information on whom is stored in a particular system. For example, the 1981 Convention stipulates that any person has the right to know about the existence of a data file about him/her, as well as data about the controller of the file; to receive, after a reasonable period of time and without unreasonable delay or excessive expenditure, confirmation of whether the data relating to him is stored in the corresponding file, and a copy of the file; seek to correct or destroy data if they have been processed in violation of the domestic legislation adopted on the basis of the 1981 Convention; etc.

For the regional level, there is a trend towards harmonization with regard to automatic processing of personal data. This trend is manifested not just in EU acts but also in the OECD Guidelines of 1980. The second part of this document contains basic principles for application on the national level. They are named the Collection Limitation Principle, the Data Quality Principle, the Purpose Specification Principle, the Use Limitation Principle, etc. For example, the Collection Limitation Principle means that there should be limits to the collection of personal data and any such data should be obtained by lawful and fair means and, where appropriate, with the knowledge or consent of the data subject.

It is characteristic that the OECD document is different from the Convention for the Protection of Individuals with regard to Automatic Processing of Personal Data of 1981. For example, the 1981 Convention does not include the Openness Principle, which means that there must be a policy of openness to achievements, practices, and measures regarding personal data. However, the other principles are essentially the same.

The existing international documents concerning the protection of personal data as a component of privacy protection ultimately aim at harmonization of the national legislation of the individual states. They have limited coverage of international cooperation issues with consideration of the traditional forms of cooperation between states.

In particular, the OECD Guidelines stipulate that OECD Member countries should establish procedures to facilitate information exchange related to these Guidelines, and mutual assistance in the procedural and investigative matters involved. This document does not contain any more specific provisions.

More specific procedures for mutual assistance are contained in the 1981 Convention. This Convention stipulates that each Party shall designate one or more authorities for assistance in order to implement this Convention, the name and address of which it shall communicate to the Secretary General of the Council of Europe; the designated authorities shall receive requests for assistance from the authorities of other states and act on such requests.

On November 8, 2001, an Additional Protocol to the 1981 Convention was signed, which contains important provisions on supervisory authorities to be established by each state that is a party to the Convention. Each party provides one (or more) supervisory authority that is responsible for enforcing the restrictions of national law, ensuring the implementation of the principles set out in Chapters II and III of the 1981 Convention and the Protocol. To this purpose, these bodies, in particular, authorize to conduct investigations and intervene in legal processes, as well as take part in them or focus the attention of the competent judicial authorities on the violation of national law. Each supervisory authority considers claims signed by any person regarding the protection of his rights and fundamental freedoms with regard to the processing of personal data.

The system of supervisory authorities, which is being established since 2001, assists both interstate cooperation and protection of the rights of the data subject. The possibility for private individuals to apply to the supervisory authorities with regard to the protection of their personal data enables transborder cooperation related to the protection of personal data. In essence, the system of supervisory authorities is the prototype of an international privacy protection network. Another significant fact is that the competence of the authorities includes powers of investigation and intervention in jurisdiction proceedings.

The 1981 Convention also contains a special procedure of assistance to data subject's resident abroad. In the framework of this procedure, where a data subject resides on the territory of another party, he or she shall be given the option of submitting the request through the intermediary of the supervisory authority designated by that party.

Therefore, issues of mutual assistance regulated by the 1981 Convention take consideration of the interests of individuals whose data can be resided in other states. This contributes to development of the institution of legal assistance, allowing it to be provided by the authorized bodies on the request of individuals in the framework of an administrative procedure. This experience should be adopted on the universal level.

However, the development of the legal foundations of the global information society is largely spontaneous. The institutional mechanism of cooperation between the states is lacking a systemic vision of what legal regulation should be appropriate for the development of scientific and technical progress.

On the universal level, it is necessary to establish the legal foundations of the global information society.

It should be noted that at present, proposals on the conclusion of universal international treaties are primarily made by nonstate actors. The International Conference of Data Protection and Privacy Commissioners adopted a resolution entitled "The Standards of Privacy and Personal Data", under which it established a working group on the development of a draft universal treaty and specified the criteria for the development of such a draft. It is planned to submit the developed articles of the treaty to the UN. Therefore, researchers and international forums are proposing detailed projects, while no systemic work is done in the framework of the UN, WIPO, ITU, and UNESCO.

5. Conclusion

Information and communication systems as complex objects of intellectual property need legal protection on the universal level. They have different functional assignment. Artificial intelligence is an information and communication system capable of synthesizing creative activity in the literary, artistic, and industrial fields. Big data is an information and communication system capable of collecting and processing information and providing access to it, in particular, with engagement of artificial intelligence. However, these objects are united in one category due to their complex structure. It is proposed to solve this problem by the development and adoption of an additional act to the Berne Convention for the Protection of Literary and Artistic Works of 1886, which establishes the legal regime for complex objects of copyright.

It appears quite reasonable to abolish the unification of the concept of privacy and personal data as a component of privacy in international law. Privacy is an area where individual needs of a person to be left to himself/herself are revealed. Every individual will delineate the limits of his/her privacy himself/herself. Contemporary international law is limited to regulation of matters of collection, processing, storage, and transfer of personal data, which are not the only issues of privacy. It appears that the privacy provision in the International Covenant on Civil and Political Rights is quite generalized but does not require specification in the information age, as it enables any individual to protect privacy in every case when the individual so wishes. In order to make international law a flexible privacy protection instrument that is adapted to every person's needs, it is necessary to introduce new privacy protection mechanisms through a combination of treaty and institutional mechanisms.

At present, acts adopted in the framework of universal international organizations primarily relate to public law aspects of international information security and do not cover personal privacy. On the universal level, it is necessary to unify the conflict of law provisions on privacy protection. In order to guarantee privacy on the universal level, networks can be established similarly to regional networks for the protection of consumer rights. The establishment of such networks may be based on an international treaty or a resolution of an international organization. The network can exchange information, provide assistance in dispute settlement, and facilitate the cooperation of judicial and administrative authorities.

The information society concept should be accompanied by an integral concept of international legal regulation of information exchange relations in the information society. A key priority for the universal level is solving the problems that have already been solved in the framework of the Council of Europe (combating computer crime, personal data protection, regulation of services of the information society, and providing access to official information). At the same time, problems should be solved related to access to other types of information (in the fields of economics, law, education, and science), facilitation of the use of telecommunications, primarily electronic, in all the fields of international cooperation, development of unified standards of the Internet functioning including technical standards and network use rules, combating cyber-terrorism and defamation, and protection of intellectual property in the information society.

As a possible option for solving a set of complex problems arising in the global information society, it is proposed to establish an international mechanism to coordinate the cooperation of states in the development of a legal foundation of the global information society. For this purpose, an international organization can be established on the basis of the World Summit on the Information Society. Converting it to an international organization would not be difficult, as it has never stopped its activity. Further, the World Summit may make agreements with the UN, UNESCO, ITU, and other international organizations in order to coordinate the cooperation of international organizations in the information society development.

Author details

Valentina Petrovna Talimonchik
Saint Petersburg State University, Russia

*Address all correspondence to: talim2008@yandex.ru

References

[1] Matterlart A. The Information Society: An Introduction. London: SAGE Publication Ltd; 2003. 182 p

[2] Webster F. Theories of the Information Society. 3rd ed. London: Routledge; 2006. 317 p

[3] Masuda Y. The Information Society as Post-Industrial Society. Bethesda: World Future Society; 1980. 171 p

[4] Bainbridge DI. Introduction to Information Technology Law. 6th ed. Edinburg: Pearson Education Limited; 2008. 665 p

[5] Campbell D, Ban C, editors. Legal Issues in the Global Information Society. New York: Oceana Publications Inc.; 2005. 758 p

[6] Rowland D, Macdonald E. Information Technology Law. 3rd ed. Abingdon: Cavendish Publishing Ltd; 2005. 573 p

[7] Lloyd IJ. Information Technology Law. 5th ed. Oxford: Oxford University Press; 2008. 597 p

[8] Murray A. Information Technology Law: Law and Society. Oxford: Oxford university press; 2010. 596 p

[9] Lashbrooke EC. Legal reasoning and artificial intelligence. Loyola Law Review. 1988;**34**:287-310

[10] Blodget N. Artificial intelligence comes of age. ABA Journal. 1987;**73**(1):68

[11] Shuller AL. At the crossroads of control: The intersection of artificial intelligence in autonomous weapon systems with international humanitarian law. Harvard National Security Journal. 2017;**8**:379-425

[12] Sarfaty GA. Can big data revolutionize international human rights law. University of Pennsylvania Journal of International Law. 2017;**39**(1):73-102

[13] Fuller R. Structuring big data to facilitate democratic participation in international. International Journal of Legal Information. 2014;**42**(3):504-516

[14] Hashiguchi M. The global artificial intelligence revolution challenges patent eligibility laws. Journal of Business & Technology Law. 2017;**13**(1):1-35

[15] Jehoram TC. Copyright in non-original writings past-present-future? In: Kabel J, Mom G, editors. Intellectual Property and Information Law. Essays in Honour of Herman Cohen Jehoram. Hague: Kluwer Law International; 1998. p. 108

[16] Oler HL. Statutory copyright protection for electronic digital computer programs: Administrative considerations. Law and Computer Technology. 1998;**7**(4):96-116

[17] Rowland D, Kohl U, Charlesworth A. Information Technology Law. 5th ed. London: Routledge; 2017. 549 p

Chapter 4

Prediction of Cancer Patient Outcomes Based on Artificial Intelligence

Suk Lee, Eunbin Ju, Suk Woo Choi, Hyungju Lee, Jang Bo Shim, Kyung Hwan Chang, Kwang Hyeon Kim and Chul Yong Kim

Abstract

Knowledge-based outcome predictions are common before radiotherapy. Because there are various treatment techniques, numerous factors must be considered in predicting cancer patient outcomes. As expectations surrounding personalized radiotherapy using complex data have increased, studies on outcome predictions using artificial intelligence have also increased. Representative artificial intelligence techniques used to predict the outcomes of cancer patients in the field of radiation oncology include collecting and processing big data, text mining of clinical literature, and machine learning for implementing prediction models. Here, methods of data preparation and model construction to predict rates of survival and toxicity using artificial intelligence are described.

Keywords: big data, artificial intelligence, prediction, cancer patient outcomes, radiation oncology

1. Introduction

1.1 Definitions of big data

There are numerous definitions of big data covering attributes from technological needs to key thresholds to social impacts [1]. One popular definition of big data, proposed by Gartner, encompasses the "3Vs: volume, velocity, and variety" [2]. This definition refers to the increasing size of standard datasets, the increasing rate at which they are produced, and the increasing range of formats and representations employed. But there are few numerical quantifications in place to analyze big data. A fourth V, veracity, was added by IBM in 2012 [3]. Veracity describes questions of trust and uncertainty regarding data and results stemming from data. De Mauro et al. proposed an alternative definition of big data, introducing a fifth V (value): "Big data is the information asset characterized by such a high volume, velocity, and variety as to require specific technology and analytical methods for its transformation into value" (**Figure 1**) [1].

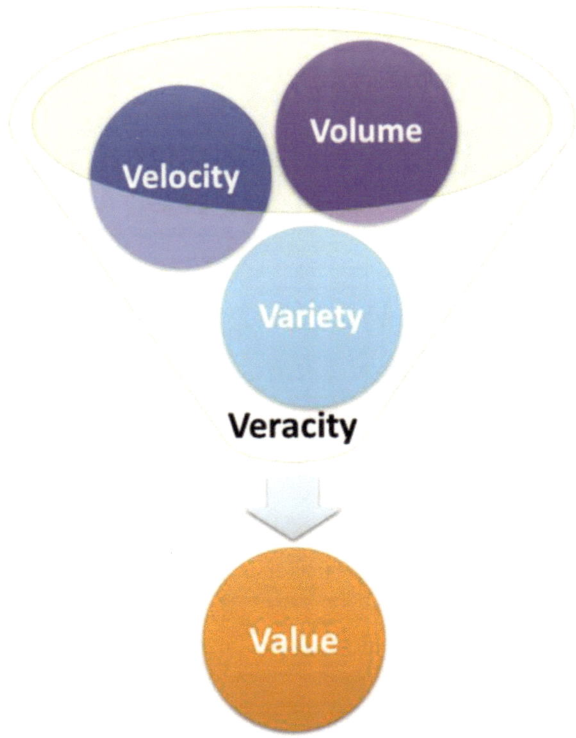

Figure 1.
The 5 Vs of big data [4].

1.2 Differences between statistical analyses and machine learning

Statistical analyses are traditionally conducted using a mathematical formula based on a hypothesis, whereas machine learning is algorithm-based using data without rule-based programming. Statistics aims to infer the relationship between input and output and can explain the outcome of a probability distribution when the hypothesis is satisfied. A predictive model using statistical analyses has high explanatory power but low predictive power. Traditional statistical methods thus depend on a hypothesis. In most cases, machine learning predicts by directly modeling and learning from data, without hypothesis-based or rule-based programming. Machine learning focuses on important features; it ignores noise and outliers by extracting only important features from the data for the predictive model (**Figure 2**).

1.3 Big data in healthcare

Medical big data comprises complex results from a diversity of diseases, treatment methods, outcomes, data resources, analytical methods, and approaches for collecting, processing, and interpreting data [5]. There are various sources of medical big data, such as hospital information systems (HIS), electronic medical records (EMR), order communication records (OCR), picture archiving and communication systems (PACS), patient reports, biomarker data, genomic data, prospective cohort studies, and large clinical trials [6, 7]. There are several distinctive features of medical data that are different from data in other fields. Medical

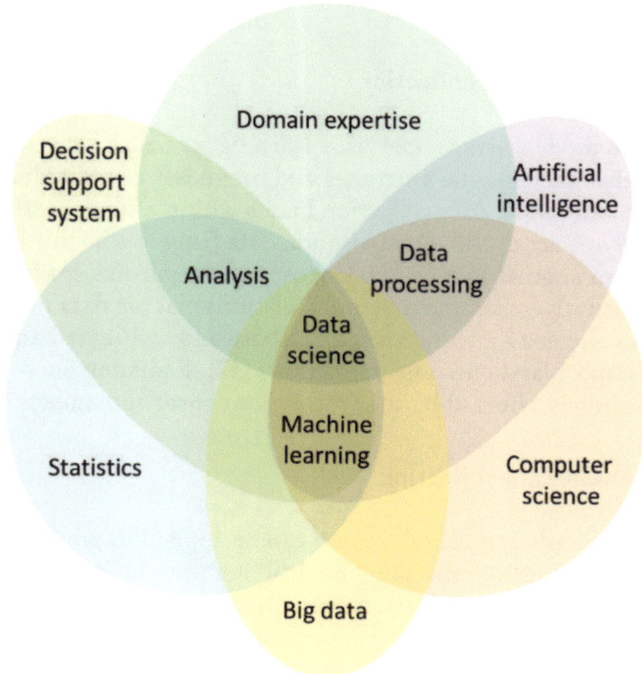

Figure 2.
The field of data science including statistics, big data, and artificial intelligence [8].

data are often difficult to access. Many investigators in the medical field are hesitant to practice open data science for various reasons, including the risk of data misuse by other parties. Medical data are often collected based on established protocols. These protocols commonly include preprocessing to simplify raw data. Both the acquisition and sharing of medical data require institutional approvals (e.g., approvals from an institutional review board), privacy protection for patients, shared agreement over the meaning of certain data elements, and an overall technology infrastructure enabling data sharing (such as a cloud-based system).

1.4 Big data in radiation oncology

In the radiation oncology field, diagnostic and therapeutic data are acquired throughout the course of treatment and during follow-up. Specific to radiation oncology, heterogeneous and voluminous amounts of data must be evaluated. These data exist in different formats across various information systems. Examples include hospital, laboratory, and oncology information systems (HIS, LIS, OIS), picture archiving and communication systems (PACS), and systems to record and verify (R&V) [9]. As expectations for personalized radiotherapy using complex data have increased, studies on outcome predictions using artificial intelligence have also increased. Specifically, studies of decision support systems based on big data have increased [10–12]. Several decision support systems have been developed in radiation oncology. Decision support systems for treatment planning have integrated imaging, dosimetry, biological, and other data in a quantitative manner to provide specific clinical predictions [13]. For example, a treatment planning decision support system that predicts radiation toxicity based on big data now exists [14]. Importantly, validation and standardization are crucial when developing medical decision support systems [15, 16].

2. Data preparation

2.1 Multi-institutional data collection

For prediction models using supervised learning, patient's data can be obtained by retrospectively analyzing the outcomes and prognoses of individual cancer patients. Since there can be data collection biases within a single institution, multi-institutional analyses are useful. Furthermore, data from one institution can be used to verify data from another institution. Oncospace (http://oncospace.radonc.jhmi.edu/) is a representative example of a multi-institutional big data platform in the field of radiation oncology. It comprises a database and web-based analysis tools for planning, data import, and outcome predictions [17]. Radiation oncology data sharing has been positively affected by the Oncospace consortium model.

2.2 Literature-based data collection

Data from previously published sources can be applied to prediction models. Representative databases for searching medical literature include PubMed (www.ncbi.nlm.nih.gov./entrez/query.fcgi), ScienceDirect (www.sciencedirect.com), Scirus (www.scirus.com/srsapp), ISI Web of Knowledge (http://www.isiwebofknowledge.com), and Google Scholar (http://scholar.google.com). It is important to obtain as many relevant studies as possible, as loss of studies can lead to bias.

The PRISMA statement recommends that a full electronic search of at least one major database be included [18]. Database searches can be augmented with manual searches of relevant papers, books, abstracts, and conference proceedings. Cross-checking references, capturing citations in review papers, and including communications from scientists working in a relevant field are important methods used to ensure that a comprehensive search is conducted [19].

3. Definitions of cancer patient outcomes

In 1993, the Outcomes Working Group (OWG) of the American Society of Clinical Oncology (ASCO) defined the outcomes of cancer treatment to be used for technical assessment and the development of cancer treatment guidelines [20]. According to the OWG, patient outcomes (e.g., survival rate or quality of life) should be prioritized over cancer outcomes (e.g., toxicity, response, or cost-effectiveness). Since a single outcome is not indicative of the overall patient outcome following cancer treatment, multiple outcomes should be considered [20]. In this chapter, we discuss three important outcomes to consider when choosing a treatment plan: toxicity, response, and survival rate.

3.1 Toxicity

Toxicity (either acute or chronic) is vitally important, with chronic toxicity being particularly critical in children [20]. The Radiation Therapy Oncology Group (RTOG) distinguishes acute and late toxicity from the side effects that occur during radiation therapy and provides guidelines for the clinical management of toxicity graded for each critical organ. Toxicity can be scored using the Common Terminology Criteria for Adverse Events (CTCAE). The CTCAE scoring system is a product of the US National Cancer Institute (NCI) [21]. Toxicity is graded as mild (grade 1), moderate (grade 2), severe (grade 3), or life-threatening (grade 4), with specific parameters for the organ system involved. Death (grade 5) is used to denote a fatality occurring during treatment [22].

3.2 Response

A solid tumor response assessment usually consists of a bidimensional (World Health Organization criteria, WHO) or unidimensional (response evaluation criteria in solid tumors guidelines, RECIST) measurement of tumors before and after chemotherapy [23, 24].

A treatment response can be grouped into four categories which are as follows: a complete response (CR), with the disappearance of all target lesions; a partial response (PR), with a decrease of greater than 30% of the target lesions; disease progression (DP), with an increase of greater than 20% of the target lesions, the appearance of new lesions, and/or the unequivocal progression of nontarget lesions; and stable disease (SD), with changes in tumor size not otherwise qualifying as PR or PD [23, 25].

3.3 Survival rate

The 5-year survival rate represents the percentage of patients living at least 5 years after a cancer is found. For example, the international 5-year survival rate for patients with lung cancer varies from 5–16% [26].

4. Prediction models

The accurate prediction of a patient's outcome before radiotherapy is an interesting and challenging task (**Figure 3**) [15, 28–30]. Machine learning (ML) methods have become popular with medical researchers. ML techniques can discover and identify patterns and relationships between treatment methods and outcomes. Using complex datasets, ML algorithms are increasingly able to predict outcomes for a specific cancer type [16, 29, 31–34].

The artificial neural net (ANN) and support vector machine (SVM) classifiers are among the most widely used ML algorithms related to cancer patient outcomes. The ANN algorithm has been used for almost 30 years. The SVM tool constitutes a more recent approach to predict cancer outcomes and is popular for its accurate

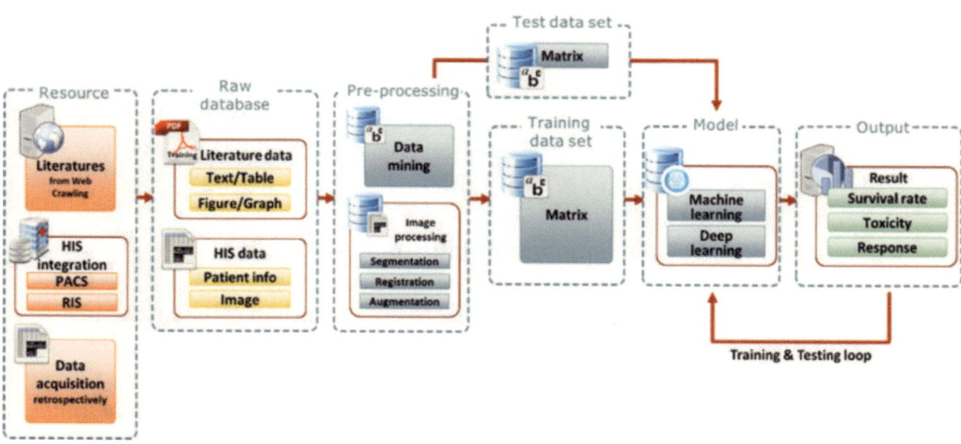

Figure 3.
Workflow of a prediction model, from raw data to the prediction result [27].

predictive performance. The most suitable algorithm choice for prediction depends on various parameters, including the type of data collected, the size of the data samples, the time frame for collection and analysis, and the type of results needed [29].

When using literature to collect data for prediction model implementation, text mining is often needed to transform literature to structured data. A major part of the text mining process involves the crucial stage of preprocessing the literature (i.e., dealing with unstructured data). Preprocessing techniques such as text categorization and term extraction are necessary. The text mining process itself requires the storage of intermediate representations, techniques to analyze intermediate representations, clustering, trend analysis, association rules, and visualization of results [35].

4.1 Toxicity prediction using clinical data

When treating cancer patients, the dual administration of chemotherapy and radiotherapy can cause severe toxicity [36]. Several studies using ANN to predict the toxicity of radiation therapy at various tumor sites have been conducted. Among tumor sites, there is a high probability of radiation toxicity in the head and neck. According to one study in 2002, they tested on clinical data and proved to be able to predict which patients will tolerate a combined chemoradiotherapy and to supply a potential predictive indicator for radiation toxicity. Clinical data were derived from 63 consecutive cases. All patients admitted into the study received induction chemotherapy for three cycles followed by concomitant chemoradiotherapy to treat head and neck cancer. They used an interval arithmetic perceptron (IAP) algorithm that consists of a neural network with a single layer of weights. The prediction performance using 11 input variables is 76.19% of correctly classified cases, whereas the whole network using 38 input variables allows only 53.97% of successes, confirming that reducing the input variables to the salient ones do improve statistical performances [37].

4.2 Response prediction using medical images

To better predict tumor responses to chemotherapy, a modeling study using CT and MR images was performed. In breast cancer patients, MR images generated useful clinical markers. MR images of 68 cancer patients were obtained before neoadjuvant chemotherapy, after which 25 patients were CR and 43 were NR. There is no statistically significant difference of each of these image features between the CR and NR case groups ($p > 0.05$). After applying ROC analysis on each of the 39 features, 10 features yielded AUC > 0.6 in classifying between the CR and NR case groups. The artificial neural network yielded an $AUC = 0.96 \pm 0.03$, which is significantly higher than $AUC = 0.85 \pm 0.05$ yielded using a simple feature fusion method ($p < 0.01$). The overall accuracy of response prediction was 94% with a sensitivity of 88% at a specificity of 98% [38].

4.3 Survival rate prediction using immunohistochemical data

In 2003, an ANN analysis proved to be more accurate than a statistical analysis in predicting the survival rate of patients with non-small cell lung cancer (NSCLC). In the study, a predictive model was implemented using data from 125 lung cancer patients. The study used 17 input variables (including five immunohistochemical parameters: p27 percentage, p27 intensity, p53, cyclin D1, and retinoblastoma) and 12 clinicopathological variables (including age, sex, smoking index, tumor size, p factor, pT, pN, stage, and histology). The prediction accuracy of the NSCLC 5-year survival rate using ANN was 87%, whereas the prediction accuracy using a logistic regression analysis was 78% [39].

4.4 Text mining-based toxicity prediction model

Prediction of radiation toxicity at the treatment planning stage of radiotherapy can improve tumor control and quality of life. However, due to the lack of patient data analyzed retrospectively in actual clinical practice, there is a limit to establish accurate prediction models. Thus, we used semantic data mining method to structure the meta-analysis literature related to radiation pneumonitis and constructed a dataset for machine learning. The 160 peer-reviewed papers related to radiation pneumonitis were structured through semantic data mining (Konan Analytics 4, Konan Technology Inc., Republic of Korea). In a structured learning dataset, the target variable was set to grade 1–5 pneumonitis graded according to the National Cancer Institute Common Toxicity Criteria version 3.0. The predictor variable was set to 10 factors (interstitial lung disease, chronic obstructive pulmonary disease, pulmonary function, age, concurrent chemotherapy, tumor location, mean lung dose, V15, V20, V30). Based on the target variable characteristics, support vector regression algorithm was implemented using the scikit-learn open source toolkit. The accuracy of the regression model was expressed in the form of root-mean-square error (RMSE) comparing the difference between the predicted value and the actual value. In order to evaluate the results of radiation pneumonitis prediction using unstructured data, we compared structured data that retrospectively analyzed 110 cases of lung cancer patients. Therefore, the semantic database of 39,404 cases related to radiation pneumonitis was constructed through semantic data mining. The results of the radiation pneumonitis prediction showed RMSE of 1.307 using a structured semantic database and RMSE of 1.056 using the retrospectively analyzed lung cancer patient data. It was confirmed that there is no difference between prediction model using unstructured data and structured data (RMSE cost difference, 0.251).

5. Limitations

The main obstacle to widely applying AI in the radiation oncology field is the lack of valid data. Only 2–3% of available data adequately capture a patient's current state of health and medical history. Suitable data are, nonetheless, included in certain ongoing clinical trials.

Since no dataset is likely to include all the features needed for an AI analysis, handling of missing data is needed to build a sufficient dataset for machine learning. A researcher can compensate for missing data by interpolating from the surrounding values, filling gaps with average values, or applying new artificial intelligence methods. The "curse of dimension" seen in machine learning with numerous features may make it necessary to select input factors using techniques like principal component analysis (PCA) or feature selection.

6. Conclusions

Due to the increasing size of datasets, the increasing rate at which they are produced and the increasing range of formats employed, predictive analysis studies using big data and artificial intelligence have also increased. In the radiation oncology field, there are ongoing trials to implement AI for predictive analyses.

Outcomes such as survival rate, tumor response, and radiation toxicity are important to cancer patients and physicians alike. In some cases, ANN is superior to conventional statistical analyses in predicting a cancer patient's prognosis. Recently, an ensemble model has emerged, combining the advantages of various ML algorithms to make predictions. Although it is sometimes difficult to interpret the processes and results obtained from artificial intelligence techniques, the current research into explainable artificial intelligence (XAI) can help to provide insight [40]. Given the lack of retrospectively analyzed data, there are limits to collecting learning data of high quality. This limitation might be overcome by data mining the clinical literature. In summary, the increased use of big data and complex variables in medicine suggests that AI will become increasingly crucial in predicting cancer patient outcomes.

Acknowledgements

This project was supported by the Korean Small and Medium Business Administration (Grant No. C0558199 and No. C0558032), the Ministry of Science, ICT and Future Planning in Korea (2017R1A2B2004012), and Korea University (K1722451).

Conflict of interest

The researcher claims no conflicts of interest.

Author details

Suk Lee[1*], Eunbin Ju[1], Suk Woo Choi[2], Hyungju Lee[3], Jang Bo Shim[1], Kyung Hwan Chang[4], Kwang Hyeon Kim[5] and Chul Yong Kim[1]

1 Department of Radiation Oncology, College of Medicine, Korea University, Seoul, Republic of Korea

2 Medical Standard Co., Ltd., Gyeonggi, Republic of Korea

3 Konan Technology Inc., Seoul, Republic of Korea

4 Department of Radiation Oncology, Yonsei Cancer Center, Yonsei University College of Medicine, Seoul, Republic of Korea

5 Proton Therapy Center, National Cancer Center, Gyeonggi, Republic of Korea

*Address all correspondence to: sukmp@korea.ac.kr

References

[1] Andrea DM, Marco G, Michele G. A formal definition of big data based on its essential features. Library Review. 2016; **65**(3):122-135

[2] Douglas L. 3D Data Management: Controlling Data Volume, Velocity, and Variety. Gartner. 2001

[3] Beyer MA, Laney D. The Importance of 'Big Data': A Definition. Stamford, CT: Gartner; 2012. pp. 2014-2018

[4] Jeff. Big Data, Digital Marketing, Social Listening [Internet]. 2018. Available from: http://chinetekstrategy.com/blog/2017/12/28/social-listening-big-data [Accessed: 2018-11-05]

[5] Dinov ID. Methodological challenges and analytic opportunities for modeling and interpreting big healthcare data. Gigascience. 2016;**5**(1):12

[6] Lee CH, Yoon HJ. Medical big data: Promise and challenges. KidneyResearch and Clinical Practice. 2017;**36**(1):3-11

[7] Slobogean GP et al. Bigger data, bigger problems. Journal of Orthopaedic Trauma. 2015;**29**:S43-S46

[8] Palmer S. Data Science for the C-Suite. New York: Digital Living Press; 2015

[9] Kessel KA, Combs SE. Data management, documentation and analysis systems in radiation oncology: A multi-institutional survey. Radiation Oncology. 2015;**10**(1):230

[10] Ree A, Redalen K. Personalized radiotherapy: Concepts, biomarkers and trial design. The British Journal of Radiology. 2015;**88**(1051):20150009

[11] Lambin P et al. Decision support systems for personalized and participative radiation oncology. Advanced Drug Delivery Reviews. 2017; **109**:131-153

[12] Huilgol N. Big data in radiation oncology. Journal of Cancer Research and Therapeutics. 2016;**12**(3):1107-1108

[13] Lee S, Cao YJ, Kim CY. Physical and radiobiological evaluation of radiotherapy treatment plan. In: Evolution of Ionizing Radiation Research. Rijeka, Croatia: InTech; 2015

[14] Lee S et al. Predictive Solution for Radiation Toxicity Based on Big Data; 2017

[15] Lambin P et al. Predicting outcomes in radiation oncology–Multifactorial decision support systems. Nature Reviews. Clinical Oncology. 2013;**10**(1): 27-40

[16] Jochems A et al. Developing and validating a survival prediction model for NSCLC patients through distributed learning across 3 countries. International Journal of Radiation Oncology, Biology, Physics. 2017;**99**(2): 344-352

[17] Bowers MR et al. Oncospace consortium: A shared radiation oncology database system designed for personalized medicine and research. International Journal of Radiation Oncology Biology Physics. 2015;**93**(3): E385

[18] Moher D et al. Preferred reporting items for systematic review and meta-analysis protocols (PRISMA-P) 2015 statement. Systematic Reviews. 2015; **4**(1):1

[19] Haidich A-B. Meta-analysis in medical research. Hippokratia. 2010;**14** (Supp. 1):29

[20] Fetting J et al. Outcomes of cancer treatment for technology assessment and cancer treatment guidelines. Journal of Clinical Oncology. 1996;**14**(2): 671-679

[21] US Department of Health and Human Services. Common terminology criteria for adverse events (CTCAE) version 4.0. National Institutes of Health, National Cancer Institute. 2009;**4**(3)

[22] Savarese DM. Common Terminology Criteria for Adverse Events. UpToDate. Waltham, MA: UpToDate; 2013

[23] Shanbhogue AKP, Karnad AB, Prasad SR. Tumor response evaluation in oncology: Current update. Journal of Computer Assisted Tomography. 2010; **34**(4):479-484

[24] Park JO et al. Measuring response in solid tumors: Comparison of RECIST and WHO response criteria. Japanese Journal of Clinical Oncology. 2003; **33**(10):533-537

[25] Duffaud F, Therasse P. New guidelines to evaluate the response to treatment in solid tumors. Bulletin du Cancer. 2000;**87**(12):881-886

[26] Butler CA et al. Variation in lung cancer survival rates between countries: Do differences in data reporting contribute? Respiratory Medicine. 2006; **100**(9):1642-1646

[27] Eunbin Ju SL, Kim KH, Choi SW, Chang KH, Cao YJ, Shim JB, et al. Quantitative analysis of weight of prognostic factors related to radiation pneumonitis using statistical analysis and artificial neural network. In: American Society for Radiation Oncology(ASTRO) Annual Meeting. 2018

[28] El Naqa I et al. Predicting radiotherapy outcomes using statistical learning techniques. Physics in Medicine & Biology. 2009;**54**(18):S9

[29] Kourou K et al. Machine learning applications in cancer prognosis and prediction. Computational and Structural Biotechnology Journal. 2015; **13**:8-17

[30] Feng M et al. Machine learning in radiation oncology: Opportunities, requirements, and needs. Frontiers in Oncology. 2018;**8**:110

[31] Oermann EK et al. Using a machine learning approach to predict outcomes after radiosurgery for cerebral arteriovenous malformations. Scientific Reports. 2016;**6**:21161

[32] Jochems A et al. Distributed learning: Developing a predictive model based on data from multiple hospitals without data leaving the hospital–A real life proof of concept. Radiotherapy and Oncology. 2016;**121**(3):459-467

[33] Lustberg T et al. Implementation of a rapid learning platform: Predicting 2-year survival in laryngeal carcinoma patients in a clinical setting. Oncotarget. 2016;**7**(24):37288

[34] Lambin P et al. Rapid learning health care in oncology–An approach towards decision support systems enabling customised radiotherapy. Radiotherapy and Oncology. 2013; **109**(1):159-164

[35] Feldman R et al. Mining the biomedical literature using semantic analysis and natural language processing techniques. Biosilico. 2003;**1**(2):69-80

[36] Su M et al. An artificial neural network for predicting the incidence of radiation pneumonitis. Medical Physics. 2005;**32**(2):318-325

[37] Drago GP et al. Forecasting the performance status of head and neck cancer patient treatment by an interval arithmetic pruned perceptron. IEEE Transactions on Biomedical Engineering. 2002;**49**(8):782-787

[38] Aghaei F et al. Computer-aided breast MR image feature analysis for prediction of tumor response to chemotherapy. Medical Physics. 2015; **42**(11):6520-6528

[39] Hanai T et al. Prognostic models in patients with non-small-cell lung cancer using artificial neural networks in comparison with logistic regression. Cancer Science. 2003;**94**(5):473-477

[40] Gunning D. Explainable Artificial Intelligence (xai). Defense Advanced Research Projects Agency (DARPA), nd Web; 2017

Chapter 5

Team Exploration of Environments Using Stochastic Local Search

Ramoni O. Lasisi and Robert DuPont

Abstract

We investigate the use of *Stochastic Local Search* (SLS) technique to explore environments where agents' knowledge and the time to explore such environments are limited. We extend a work that uses evolutionary algorithms to evolve teams in simulated environments. Our work proposes a formalization of the concept of state and neighborhood for SLS and provides evaluation of agents' teams using number of interesting cells. Further, we modify the environments to include goals that are randomly distributed among interesting cells. Agents in this case are then required to search for goals. Experiments using teams of different sizes show the effectiveness of our technique. Teams were able to complete exploration of *more than* 70% of the environments, while in the *best cases*, they were able to complete explorations of *more than* 80% of the environments within limited time steps. These results compare with those of the previous work. It is interesting to note that all teams of agents were able to find on average all the goals in the three environments when the size of the grid is 12. This is a 100% achievement by the agents' teams. However, performance can be seen to degrade as the environments' sizes become larger.

Keywords: agents, teams, stochastic local search, state, neighborhood, environment, experiments

1. Introduction

Autonomous agents in complex environments may need to work together as *teams* to achieve desired goals. This is an important feature of most multiagent environments where individual agents lack all the required capabilities, skills, and knowledge to complete tasks alone. These environments can model real-world problem domains where agents' knowledge and available time to complete tasks in such domains are limited. Agents may thus resort to *team formation* to complete tasks. Team formation or coalition formation are simple models of short-term cooperation [1, 2] where agents complete specific tasks.

Examples of team formation can be found in *business* (e.g., organizations forming teams to make more sales and hence, more profits), in *academia* (e.g., professors forming teams to publish articles), in *search and rescue* (e.g., robotic agents forming teams in large natural disaster environments to save life and property), and in *network security* (e.g., agents forming teams to determine critical points where checkpoints should be placed in a network to hinder adversaries' communication or movement). Since our mundane day to day activities are not exempted from team formation, we cooperate with others to solve problems that may be otherwise difficult for us to complete alone. A number of factors can be attributed to this difficulty, including time criticality of tasks, distribution of individual skills and resources, the need for an agent's presence in multiple work places simultaneously, and many more. An interesting number of works have employed various forms of team formation and search strategies in solving problems related to search or exploration. See for example the works of [3–9].

Here is a straightforward motivation for the problem we study. Consider a rescue operation in an aircraft crash site where search for survivors may be guaranteed in the first few hours of the crash. Agents neither know where survivors are located nor have enough time to explore the environment for victims. They need, preferably as teams, to devise methods that systematically explore the environment to achieve the desired goal. It is not difficult to see that this example and many other similar real-world domains can be modeled as that of *search problems*. This obviously raises the following important question: *How can teams of agents efficiently explore relatively difficult environments using appropriate search strategies that achieve acceptable outcomes?* This research provides an investigation of the use of *Stochastic Local Search* (SLS) technique to explore complex environments where agents' knowledge and the time to explore such environments are limited. We model the problem as that of an instance of a *search problem* and develop SLS techniques that enable intelligent exploration of such relatively difficult environments by teams of agents.

SLS algorithms have made significant success in solving many hard problems [10] which involve search of well-defined solutions spaces (or states). A model of SLS algorithms is defined to include a *neighborhood* and an *evaluation function*—both of which are specific to different problems. The goal of an agent using SLS algorithm is to seek a state s from the set of possible states S in the problem domain that optimizes some measures [11]. A neighborhood, $N(s)$, is defined for each state s. $N(s)$ is the set of all possible *successor states* that are local to s i.e., the set of all possible states that an agent transits into from the current state s. The evaluation function is defined to exploit the current knowledge of the neighborhood and then *stochastically* selects a successor state $s' \in N(s)$. This simple method of choosing the successor state by the evaluation function may further be guided towards solutions that optimize goals measures using heuristics. The neighborhood and evaluation function capture two interesting features of SLS algorithms that we exploit in this work.

We model the problem described in the motivation above by using three different two-dimensional grids to represent environments that agents need to explore. Some cells within the grids are referred to as being "interesting," such as *possibly* having victims in them. We then randomly distribute *goals* among the interesting cells. Goals in this work represent some desirable situation that we want agents to achieve. In the motivation above, the presence of a victim in an interesting cell will represent a goal. The three environments are further constrained such that not all interesting cells contain goals, thus agents do not have background knowledge of the environments. Agents in our model are required to devise techniques to search and find as many goals within a limited amount of time steps. The performance of agents in these environment are evaluated based on a number of factors, including the amount of goals found with respect to the number of agents in teams, type, and size of environments. The main contributions of this work are as follows:

1. We provide a formalization of the *concept of state and neighborhood* in three different simulated *random*, *clumped*, and *linear* environments described in [12].

2. We provide agents performance evaluation in the three environments using the number of interesting cells found by teams as done in [12] and our previous work [13]. We further modify the environments to include limited number of goals that are randomly distributed among the interesting cells. Agents in this case are thus required to search for goals rather than interesting cells as done in [12, 13].

3. We model agents, their methods of movements in the environments, and provide a clever design of an *evaluation function* that agents can use to navigate the three environments.

4. Finally, we provide an implementation of a model that allows agents to operate on these environments using the proposed evaluation function.

Several simulations to mimic real-world environments were completed using different dimensions of the three environments and varying agents' team sizes. The results of these simulations compare favorably with those of a previous work that was used as a benchmark. In particular, the proposed model avoids such expensive cost of extensive time requirements of evolutionary learning by agents. This is made possible as agents in this model are not subjected to training before being deployed to the testing environments. They only conduct local searches of the environments from their current locations using two important features from the SLS algorithms: neighborhood and evaluation function.

2. Related work

SLS algorithms have been successfully applied to many hard problems including Traveling Salesman Problem, Graph Coloring Problem, Satisfiability Problem in Propositional Logic, and more [10, 14]. Common SLS algorithms include *simulated annealing*, *hill climbing*, and evolutionary inspired *genetic algorithms* [15]. As highlighted in the previous section, the definitions of a neighborhood and its associated evaluation function in SLS algorithms are specific to the problem domain. The real *novelty* in the employment of SLS techniques to construct an algorithm comes from how elegant the neighborhood and the evaluation function are defined for the problem domain such that the algorithm is well-guided towards feasible solutions within a short period of time.

Soule and Heckendorn [12] describe three environments on which their work is based. We reproduce these environments and their descriptions since we have used them to evaluate our proposed SLS technique. Each of the three environments is composed of two-dimensional grids of 45×45 containing some percentages of *interesting* cells that are distributed in some ways within the environments. A cell is said to be *interesting* if it contains some sub-goals or information that leads to the desired goal of a team. Using the example of the previous section, a cell in this case will be *interesting* if it contains, say, a survivor or victim from a crash.

The environments are named according to how the number of interesting cells are distributed in the grids. They are referred to as *random*, *clumped*, and *linear*.

Figures 1–3 depict sample schematic views of random, clumped, and linear environments for a 45 × 45 two-dimensional grids. The interesting cells in each environments are shown shaded. In a random environment, each cell has a uniform 20% chance of being interesting. For clumped environment, exactly 20% of the cells are interesting and are stochastically clumped in the four corners of the grids. Finally, in the linear environment, exactly 10% of the cells are interesting and they are distributed randomly along eleven rows in the environment. The same eleven rows are always used, but the exact placement of interesting cells within the rows is random. These environments model applications in the real-world. An environment

Figure 1.
A schematic view of a random environment for a 45 × 45 two-dimensional grid.

Figure 2.
A schematic view of a clumped environment for a 45 × 45 two-dimensional grid.

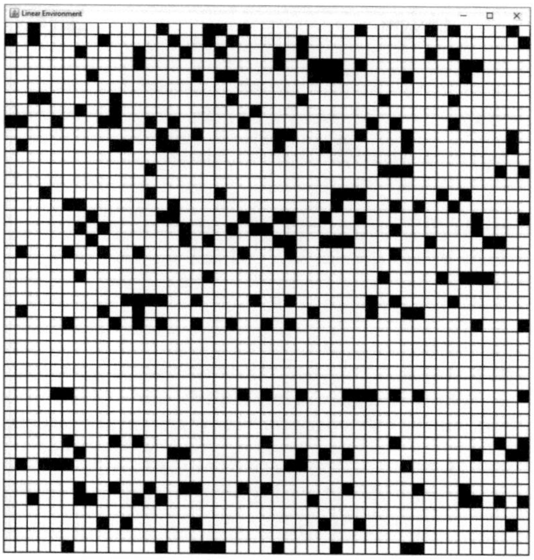

Figure 3.
A schematic view of a linear environment for a 45 × 45 two-dimensional grid.

might represent a minefield with the interesting cells representing positions of potential mines or geological formations [12]. Teams evolved to explore environments may also represent automated planetary surveying team [5].

Soule and Heckendorn use evolutionary algorithms to implement a multiagent team training algorithm called *Orthogonal Evolution of Teams* (*OET*) to *evolve* teams of agents. The three environments above alternatively serve as both the *training* and *testing* environments to evaluate the performance of their OET algorithm. They consider evolution of *heterogeneous* multiagent teams (i.e., teams of agents with specialized roles). There are two types of specialized agents in their work: *scouts* and *investigators*. The scouts and investigators are respectively responsible for finding as much as possible interesting cells and marking them as investigated. Unlike our approach however, where all agents are limited to moves of *length one* in a single time step in the environments, the scouts are allowed a move of *length two* in a single time step. Results from our work using SLS technique to explore different environments compare with those of Soule and Heckendorn's with performances within similar ranges. However, it is not yet clear how fair that comparison can be justified since their work employs evolutionary algorithm which come with extensive time requirements of evolutionary learning and huge time and costs of training for agents before they are deployed to actual testing environments.

3. Problem formalization and solution approach

Given any of the three environments (i.e., random, linear, and clumped) described in the previous section and a number of autonomous agents (each with a limited knowledge of the environments), the problem we attempt to solve is to form teams of agents that intelligently explore as much as possible interesting cells and/or goals in the grids within a limited amount of time. Our attempt in solving this problem uses a model that employs techniques from SLS algorithms. We provide in this section, a formalization of the framework and implementation details for state and neighborhood, evaluation function, and a description of the simulation employed in our research.

3.1 Framework for state and neighborhood

We present our framework of the concept of *state* and *neighborhood* in any of the three environments. Denote by c_{ij} a cell in any grid of an environment where $i, j \in \mathbb{N}$ are the Cartesian coordinates of the cell c_{ij}.

Definition 1. *A state s with a reference cell, c_{ij}, in an environment consists of the reference cell c_{ij}, and all immediate cells $c'_{i'j'}$ from c_{ij} such that $|i - i'| = 1$ or $|j - j'| = 1$.*

It is clear from Definition 3.1 that a state is composed of a 3×3 sub-matrix within an environment when the reference cell of the state is not close to or on any of the boundary cells. Note that for any $n \times n$ two-dimensional grid of the three environments, n is a multiple of 3. This constraint allows us to correctly map states to the $n \times n$ grids. An example of a state labeled s is shown in **Figure 4** with a reference cell c_{ij}. The immediate cells from c_{ij} are shaded in gray. The set of all possible states in the problem domain constitutes the search space we seek for feasible solutions (i.e., finding goals and/or as much as possible interesting cells).

Definition 2. *The neighborhood $N(s)$ of a state s consists of all states s' that share boundary with s.*

Figure 4 shows an example of a neighborhood $N(s)$ for a state s. States s_1, s_2, s_3, and s_4 (shaded in black) all share boundary with state s. Thus, $N(s) = \{s_1, s_2, s_3, s_4\}$. The size, $|N(s)|$, of the neighborhood $N(s)$ of a state s is $2 \leq |N(s)| \leq 4$, depending on whether or not s is close to any of the boundaries of the environments. The neighborhood of any regular state within the boundaries consists of only four neighboring states as shown above. **Figure 5** shows a schematic view of some possible neighborhoods for different states with reference cells, c_{ij}. Notice how incomplete, both in the number of cells and neighbors on how some of neighborhoods were defined because of the positions of the reference cells.

3.2 Implementation of state and neighborhood

We present implementation details of the framework developed in the previous section. We provide abstraction of state and neighborhood in an environment using

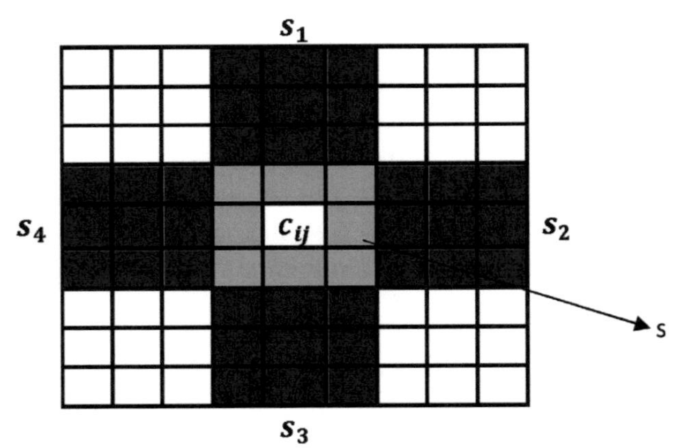

Figure 4.
A view of a state (with reference cell c_{ij}), denoted s, and a neighborhood $N(s)$ for s. $N(s) = \{s_1, s_2, s_3, s_4\}$.

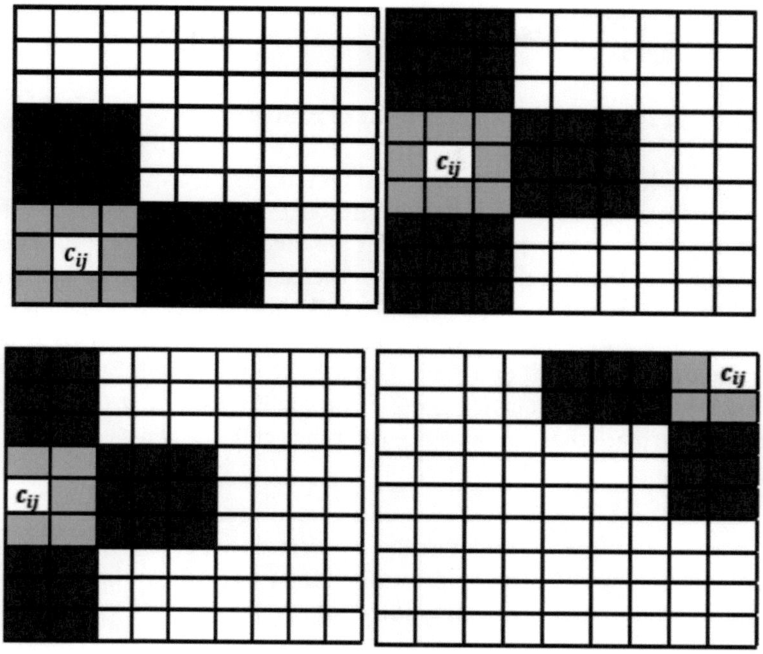

Figure 5.
A schematic view of some possible neighborhoods for different states with reference cells, c_{ij}.

the Java programming language. The following Java classes, *Cell, Agent, Environment,* and *State* are *partially* shown to include only relevant data fields and/or methods that are needed to understand the discussion of our implementation of state and neighborhood in this section.

```
public class Cell{
    //data fields
    private int x;
    private int y;
    //methods
    void setXY(int x, int y);
    int getX();
    int getY();
}
public class Agent {
    // data field
    private int[] location;
    // method
    int[] getLocation();
}
public class Environment implements Runnable {
     // data fields
    private int gridSize;
    private String [][] grid;
    private boolean [][] visitedCells;
    private Agent [] agents;
}
public class State {
    // data fields
```

```
    private int [] refCell;
    private int gridSize;
    // method
    Cell [] createCells(int [] refCell, int gridSize);
}
```

We first consider how to locate a state in an environment. Using the Agent class above, an agent is always aware of its current location. All agents start exploration of an environment from some locations that are determined randomly. These locations correspond to certain reference cells in the environment's grid. No two agents are allowed to start from the same reference cell. Since a state is made up of a 3 × 3 sub-matrix and the dimensions of an environment grid is a multiple of 3, we can exactly locate the starting cell of a state, given its reference cell. For any reference cell, $ref\ Cell[] = \{i,j\}$, i.e., a location $grid[i][j]$ in the Environment class above, the starting cell of the state that contains the reference cell is given as:

$$grid[(i/3)*3][(j/3)*3] \quad (1)$$

Thus, it is straightforward to determine the states that all the cells in the grid of an environment belongs. Given a reference cell for a state, the following provides an implementation that returns the start indices of the state.

```
public int [] getStateStartIndices(int [] refCell) {
    int i = refCell[0];
    int j = refCell[1];
    return new int [] {(i / 3) * 3, (j / 3) * 3};
}
```

When a state has been explored by an agent, the state is marked as investigated. A state is considered visited if the reference cell for the state and all of its immediate cells have been marked as investigated. Since agents are always aware of their locations, we implement this functionality for each agent using the following method:

```
public void setVisited(int [] refCell){
    if(!this.isVisited(refCell)) {
      int [] indices = getStateStartIndices(refCell);
      int x = indices[0];
      int y = indices[1];
      for(int i = x; i < gridSize && i < x + 3; i++)
        for(int j = y; j < gridSize && j < y + 3; j++)
           visitedCells[i][j] = true;
  }
}
```

Parameter *refCell* is the reference cell of the state, *gridSize* is the size of the grid, and *visitedCell* is a boolean 2-dimensional array that keeps track of cells in the grid that correspond to states already investigated by agents. We now turn attention to the implementation detail of neighborhood.

```
public State [] getNeighborhood(int [] refCell) {
    State [] neighborhood = null;
  //check top left corner
  if((refCell[0] == 0 || refCell[0] == 1) &&
        (refCell[1] == 0 || refCell[1] == 1)){
    neighborhood = new State[2];
```

```
    for(int i = 0; i < neighborhood.length; i++)
        neighborhood[i] = new State();
    //right state
    int [] s2 = {refCell[0], Math.min(refCell[1] + 3, gridSize - 1)};
    neighborhood[0].createCells(s2, gridSize);
    //bottom state
    int [] s3 = {Math.min(refCell[0] + 3, gridSize - 1), refCell[1]}; neighborhood
[1].createCells(s3, gridSize);
  }
//check left column
//check bottom left corner
//check bottom row
//check bottom right corner
//check right column
//check top right corner
//check top row
//everything else
return neighborhood;
}
```

Given the reference cell of a state, the method *getNeighborhood* above provides an implementation that determines the neighborhood of that state. The method first checks the location of the reference cell to determine the size of the neighborhood, then returns the appropriate states in the neighborhood as demonstrated in **Figure 5**. For the part of the code shown in the method, the reference cell of the state, say, s, under consideration falls on the top left corner of the grid, so only two states (i.e., the right and bottom states that share boundaries with s) are returned for the neighborhood. All other possible neighborhood are handled by the method as indicated by comments in the lower part of the method.

3.3 Evaluation function

Agents in our model use an *evaluation function* to guide selection of successor states to transit into. The evaluation function depends on the framework of the state and neighborhood we developed in the previous section. Algorithm 1 gives the pseudocode of our evaluation function.

Algorithm 1: *Successor State* $(\boldsymbol{a}, \boldsymbol{s})$.

Input: Agent a and the current state s of a.
Output: A successor state $s' \in N(s)$.

1: **procedure** *Successor* State (a, s)
2:     *SuccStates* $\leftarrow \emptyset$
3:     **for each** state $s' \in N(s)$ **do**
4:         **if** s' has not been visited **then**
5:             **if** there exists no other agent $a' \neq a$ in s' **then**
6:                 *SuccStates* $\leftarrow$ *SuccStates* $\cup \{s'\}$
7:     **if** *SuccStates* is empty **then**
8:         randomly select an s' from $N(s)$
9:     **else**
10:     randomly select an s' from *SuccStates*
11:   **return** s'
12: **end procedure**

Algorithm 1 i.e., SuccessorState (a, s) accepts two inputs—an agent a, and the current state s, of the agent. It outputs a successor state s' if one exists, otherwise it stochastically selects any state in $N(s)$ as the successor. In a single exploration of an environment by all agents in our system, each agent calls *SuccessorState*(a, s) algorithm once to determine the next state to transit into. It is not difficult to see that the total running time of a single time step of the exploration of an environment is *linear* in the number of agents, since *SuccessorState*(a, s) algorithm only examines a constant number (i.e., the four) neighboring states to s. We also show that an agent does not remain infinitely in a particular state in situations where *SuccStates* is empty, at which time the evaluation function stochastically selects any state from $N(s)$. We refer to situation where *SuccStates* is empty as a situation of "no progress". The "no progress" situation is eliminated in the next attempt by the evaluation function to find a successor state and does not occur often as described below.

Suppose an agent a is currently in a state s. Consider a certain attempt t by the evaluation function to find a successor state for a which results in a situation of "no progress". The evaluation function stochastically selects a state s' from $N(s)$ for a to transit into. Now consider the next attempt t' by the evaluation function to find a successor state for a where, as we know, the agent is currently in a new state s' following state s. Observe that the neighborhood for state s' in this attempt t' is different from the neighborhood for state s in the previous attempt t i.e., $N(s') \neq N(s)$ and s is now one of the neighboring states of s' i.e., $s \in N(s')$. Suppose again that attempt t' by the evaluation function to select a successor state for s' results in a situation of "no progress". The evaluation function again stochastically selects a state from $N(s')$. Note that the probability of selecting the state s i.e., the previous state from $N(s')$ as the successor to s' is only $\frac{1}{4}$ as against the probability $\frac{3}{4}$ of selecting any of the remaining three new states from $N(s')$.

Observe that the number of attempts required by the evaluation function until any one of the three states in $N(s')$ apart from state s is selected follows a *geometric random distribution* with probability $p = \frac{3}{4}$. Thus, the *expected* number of attempts required by the evaluation function until any one of these three states is selected is

$$p \sum_{i=1}^{\infty} i \cdot (1-p)^{i-1} = \frac{1}{p} = \frac{4}{3} < 2. \tag{2}$$

3.4 Simulation

We form teams consisting of a certain number of agents. One of the team's members is designated as a *leader*. We assume that the leader has some additional computational power than other members. The leader is responsible for maintaining an updated status (i.e., visited states) and communicates same to other members when requested. The leader answers the following queries from members: *Has a given state been visited?* and *Is there an agent in a given state?* These are the queries that are used by the evaluation function. The leader agent does not participate in the actual exploration of individual states. Other agents are responsible for locating and visiting interesting cells and as well as finding goals in the grids. All visited cells, either interesting or not, and whether goals are found or not are marked as investigated. An agent can move from her current location in only one of four directions (i.e., north, east, west, and south) and is limited to moves of *length one* in a single time step. The following three actions, goForward, turnLeft, and *turnRight* are made available to all agents except the leader.

When starting, all agents (except the leader) are randomly distributed in the environment. We describe the procedure used by agents to explore the environments next. Imagine an agent a currently in a state s that has not been visited. After the exploration of the current state, agent a invokes the evaluation function to determine the successor state to transit into. The successor state guides the decision of the agent on how it *exits* from the reference cell and the *order* it conducts the search of the current state. Having transited into a successor state, agent a determines if its current cell is interesting, and/or a goal is found, records a score, and marks the cell as visited. The agent then performs an *exhaustive search* of the immediate cells to the reference cell of state s. During the exhaustive search, the agent checks if the cells being searched are interesting, and/or goals are found, records scores as appropriate, and subsequently marks the cells as visited. On completion of the search of state s, the status of the state (i.e., visited) is communicated to the team leader.

Figure 6(a) provides a simple illustration of an agent currently in a state with reference cell x which later transits into a successor state s_4 with reference cell y.

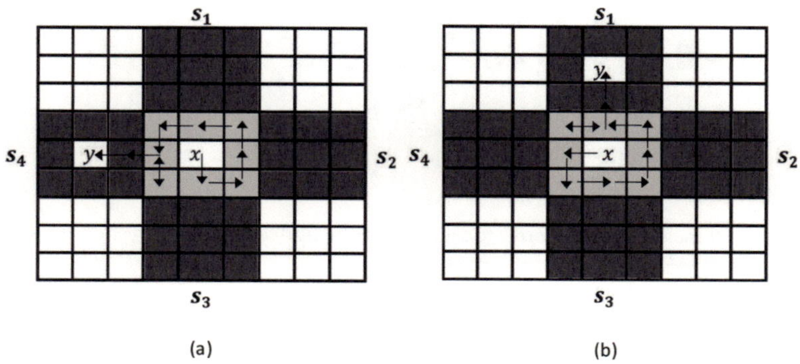

Figure 6.
Exhaustive search of a state by agents. (a) Agent exits reference cell x, search current state in the direction of the arrows, and transits into s_4 with reference y. (b) Agent exits reference cell x, search current state in the direction of arrows, and transits into s_1 with reference cell y.

Figure 7.
Random environment showing initial deployment of agents (red) and goals (yellow).

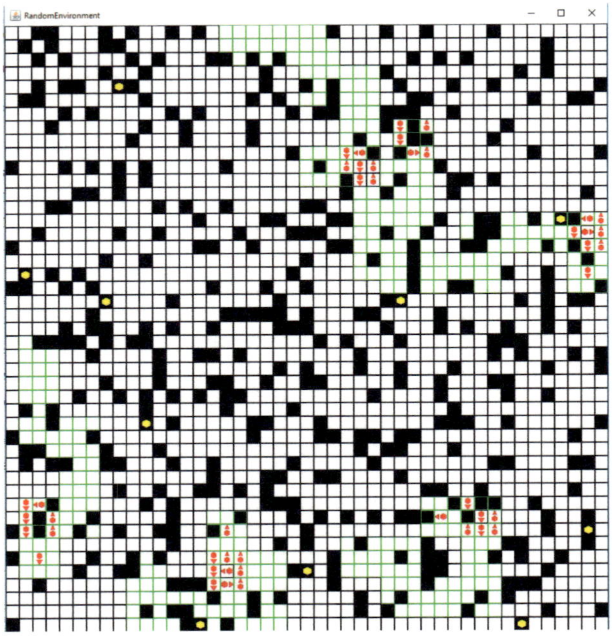

Figure 8.
Random environment showing partial search of the environment by agents. The highlighted areas covered in green have been explored by agents.

The agent first determines its successor state as s_4 using the evaluation function, then conducts an exhaustive search of the immediate cells to the reference cell x in the direction of the arrows for each time step, and finally transits into state s_4. A similar example is depicted in **Figure 6(b)** when the agent transits into state s_1 from the current state. Observe the difference in how the agents in the two figures exit the reference cells of their respective current states and the order in which they conduct their exhaustive search. This difference is due to the fact that the agents transit into different successor states from the current state. At the expiration of the exploration period, we compute the sum of the scores of interesting cells found by each agent as the total score achieved by the team of agents.

Figure 7 shows an example of a random environment with an initial deployment of six agents (red pictures with arrow heads) in the environment. There are also currently ten goals (diamond pictures in yellow) that are also randomly distributed across the grid. The agents will search the environment using the evaluation function and the concept of neighborhood proposed in this work to guide their search. A snapshot of what the search area looks like after few time steps of exploration is shown in **Figure 8**. The highlighted areas covered in green have been explored by agents, while the white areas are yet to be explored. Also, the rectangle of agents shown together illustrate an exhaustive search of that state by an agent. We make the rectangle of agents disappear in the real simulation when the agent complete exploration of the state.

4. Results and discussion

We present results of our extensive simulations in this section. Our findings are based on two different sets of experiments—first, on the percentage of interesting cells found by agents, and second, on the average number of goals found by agents in the three environments. For our study, we use a different set of parameters to include number of agents in teams, size, and type (random, linear, and clumped) of environments.

4.1 Percentage of interesting cells found by teams of agents

Figure 9 shows the average percentage of interesting cells found by six-member teams of agents for 45×45 random, clumped, and linear environments using the SLS model for 100 trials of the experiments. The corresponding standard deviations from the average percentage of interesting cells found by the agent for the three environments are also shown in **Table 1**.

The average percentage of interesting cells found by agents' teams using the SLS model provides a measure of the level of difficulty of the three environments for the teams. This conversely implies a measure of the relative performance of the teams in each of the environments. **Figure 7** shows that the relative performance of the teams in the random environment ($\sim 74\%$) is higher than that of the linear environment ($\sim 72\%$), which in turn is higher than that of the clumped environment ($\sim 68\%$). Thus, the clumped environment appears to be the most difficult of the three environments, followed by the linear, and then, the random environment. The level of difficulty in the three environments may however be assumed to be relatively close considering how small the *spread* ($74 - 68 = 6$) among the average performance of the teams in the three environments is. This is further evidenced in **Table 1** by the tightness of the standard deviations around the average percentage of interesting cells found by agents' teams in the environments.

An implication of the closeness of the level of difficulty of the three environments is that the SLS model's performance has *less reliance* on these environments. Contrarily, Soule and Heckendorn [12] have shown that the performance of the evolved teams by their model depends on both the training and testing environments. They show that training in either the random or clumped environment is a

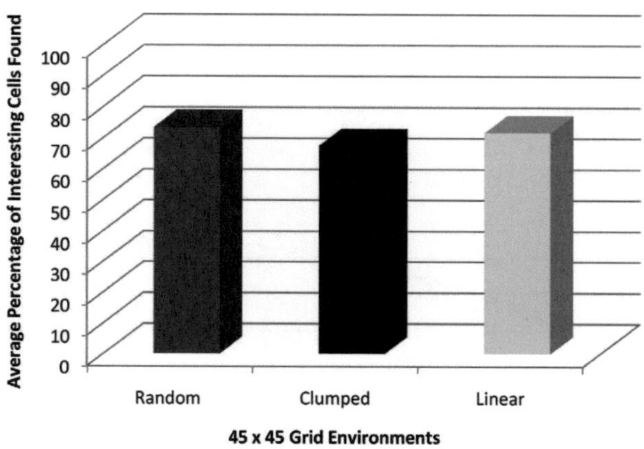

Figure 9.
Average percentage of interesting cells found by six-member teams in 45×45 *grid environments.*

	Random	Clumped	Linear
Standard deviation	1.05	1.31	1.09

Table 1.
Standard deviations from the respective average percentage of interesting cells found by six-member teams in 45×45 *grid environments.*

good training for the other environment, but neither is as good of a training environment for the linear environment. In fact, the performance of the evolved teams when they are trained in either of random or clumped, and later deployed in linear environment, is poor in comparison with when they are deployed in either the random or clumped environment. Recall also that agents in our model are not subjected to training before being deployed to the testing environments. They only conduct local searches of their environments using two important features from SLS algorithms: neighborhood and evaluation function.

For the next set of experiments, we evaluate the effectiveness of the SLS model by measuring the average percentage of interesting cells found by agents' teams, varying the number of agents in the teams, and the grid sizes in the three environments. **Figure 10** shows the average percentage of interesting cells found by agents' teams of different sizes in 45 × 45 random, clumped, and linear environments. The x-axis indicates the team member sizes while the y-axis is the average percentage of interesting cells found by these teams.

The six-member teams always discover more than 70% of the interesting cells for both the random and linear environments, and more than 65% for the clumped environment on the average. As the size of the teams increases, there is a significant increase in the average performance of the teams in the three environments. The average performance of the teams consistently increases with the teams sizes and reaching a peak value of 95% for both the random and linear environments, and 93% for the clumped environment when the team size is ten. It appears that 10-member team is the *optimal* team size when agents implement the SLS model for the three 45 × 45 grid environments. This can be confirmed from **Figure 10**.

Increasing the number of agents in the teams beyond ten does not appear to improve average performance of agents. We noticed marginal decrease in the average performance of larger teams—as teams' sizes increase past 10, the average percentage of interesting cells found drops below those of the 10-member teams. See **Figure 10** for performance of agents' teams of sizes 11 and 12 where the average percentage of interesting cells found by these teams are fairly smaller compared to those of the 10-member teams. Our explanation for this unexpected result is that as the number of agents increases, there is an increased chance of team members revisiting already visited cells. Such efforts by agents does not improve the scores (performance) of the teams since the team has already been rewarded during initial

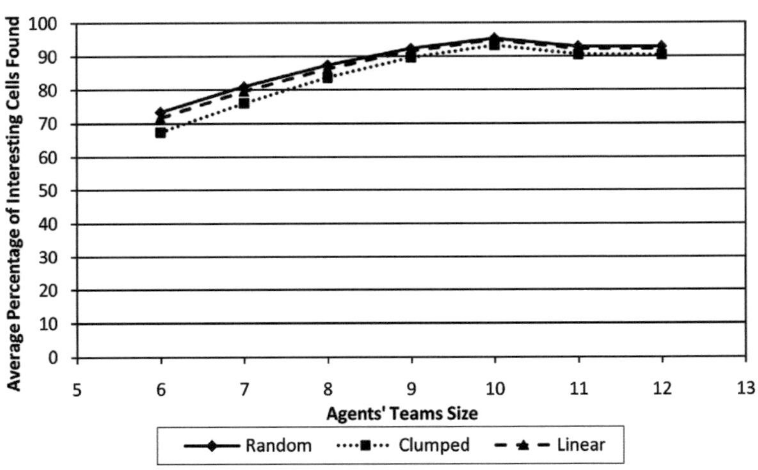

Figure 10.
Average percentage of interesting cells found by agents' teams of different sizes in 45 × 45 *grid environments.*

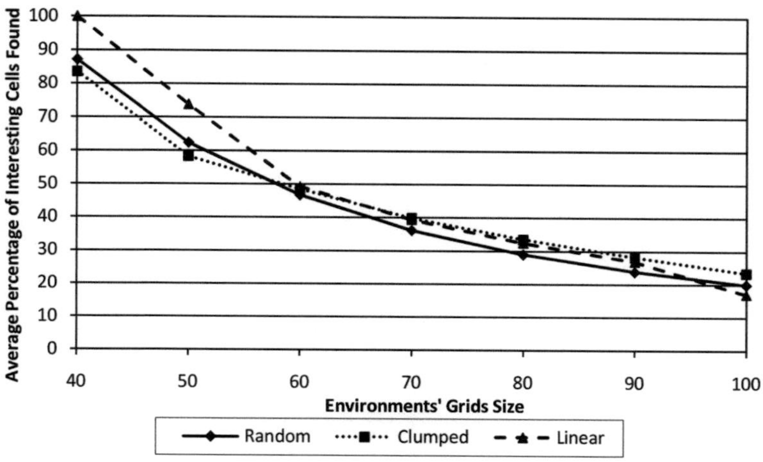

Figure 11.
Average percentage of interesting cells found by six-member teams for different grid sizes of environments.

visits of the cells by some members of the team. In other words, some agents in a team may become redundant as the size of the team becomes large.

Figure 11 shows the average percentage of interesting cells found by six-member teams for different grid sizes in the three environments. The x-axis indicates the grid sizes while the y-axis is the average percentage of interesting cells found by these teams.

The results show, perhaps not too surprising that in general, the average performance of the teams degrade for the three environments as the dimension of the grids increases. A partial explanation for this is that fixing the team size while increasing the dimension of the environments makes members of the teams to be sparsely distributed in the environments. Thus, it will then be more difficult for agents to cooperate as they now require several time steps to move closer to one another in order to cover different parts of the grids. Nonetheless, even at higher dimensions of the grids, agents' teams are still able to achieve some reasonable level of performance. For instance, when the grid size is 100×100, the 6-member teams found more than 20% of interesting cells for the random and clumped environments but below 20% for the linear environment.

4.2 Number of goals found by teams of agents

This second part of the experiments is based on the average number of goals found by agents' teams. We set the number of goals that are randomly distributed in the environments to be 10, and agents' teams are allowed to search for goals over a lifetime of 500 time steps. **Figures 12–14** respectively, show the average number of goals found by teams of agents in the random, clumped, and linear environments. The x-axes indicate the size of the grids while the y-axes are for the average number of goals found by teams. We vary team size from 1 to 5 members, and vary the grid size from 12×12 to 27×27 two-dimensional grid.

The results we observe from the figures suggest that the performance of agents' teams in the three environments are similar and consistent for agents' teams, environment types, as well as for the various grid sizes. It is interesting to see that all teams of agents were able to find on average all the 10 goals when the size of the environments is 12. This is a 100% achievement by the agents' teams. However, the performance of the teams can be seen to degrade as the size of the environments becomes larger. This degradation is expected since the agents' team sizes remain the

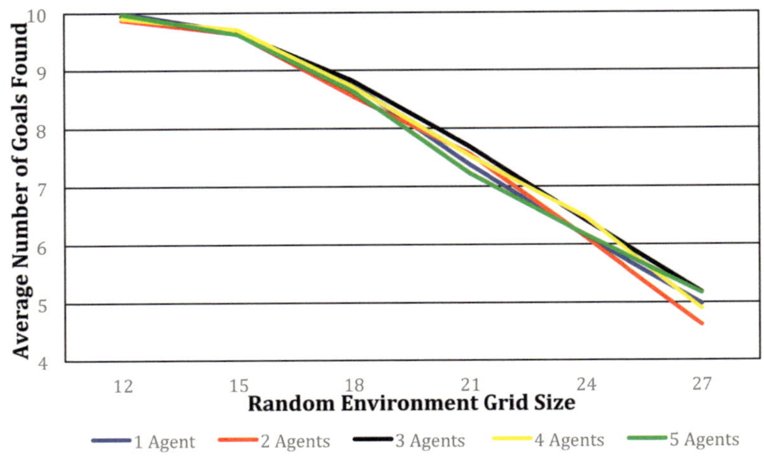

Figure 12.
Average number of goals found by agents' teams for different grid sizes in the random environment.

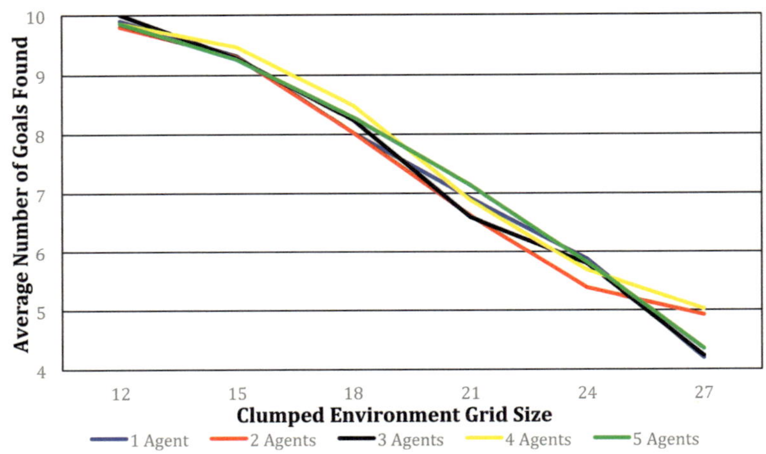

Figure 13.
Average number of goals found by agents' teams for different grid sizes in the clumped environment.

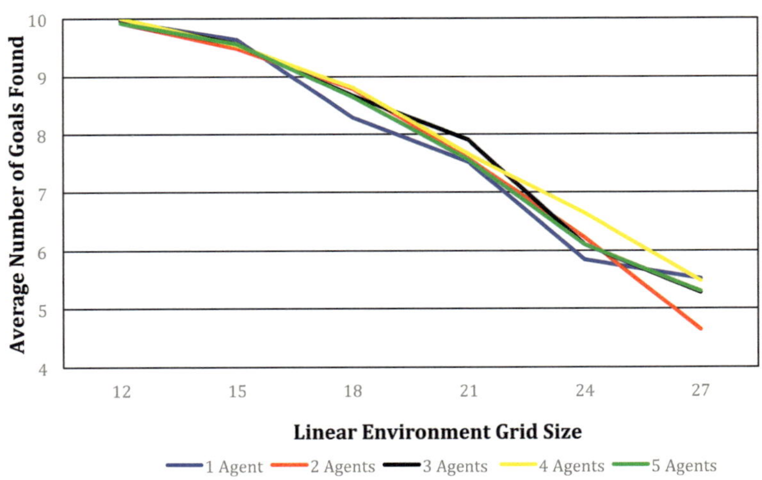

Figure 14.
Average number of goals found by agents' teams for different grid sizes in the linear environment.

same while the environments become larger. In a sense, the same number of agents need to do more work and cooperate in the larger environments. Again, these results are consistent with those of the previous section when agents are evaluated based on the percentage of interesting cells found in the environments. We note that the worst performance for all teams occurs when the size of the environments are of 27×27 dimensions. The clumped environment appears to be the most difficult in this case as all teams find less than five goals on the average.

We are interested in the lessons to be learnt from these experiments, as well as the implications of the similarity and consistency of the results across the three environments. The outcomes from these experiments suggest that our proposed SLS method is independent of the three environments, thus, agents using our search procedures are expected to perform about the same in any of the environments. This is also a confirmation of the results for agents' teams in the three environments when they are expected to find as many interesting cells from the previous section.

5. Conclusions and future work

We consider an investigation of the use of Stochastic Local Search (SLS) technique to explore complex environments where agents' knowledge and the time to explore such environments are limited. We model the problem as that of an instance of a search problem and develop a SLS technique that enables efficient exploration of such relatively difficult environments by teams of agents. Thus, we provide extensions to the work of Soule and Heckendorn [12] that uses evolutionary algorithms in evolving multiagent teams in the three different simulated random, clumped, and linear environments described in their work. We first provide a formalization of the concept of state and neighborhood in these environments and provide agents' performance evaluations in the three environments using the number of interesting cells found by teams as done in [12] and our previous work [13]. We further modify the environments to include a limited number of goals that are randomly distributed among the interesting cells. Agents in this case are thus required to search for goals rather than interesting cells.

Experiments using agents' teams of different sizes implementing our model in different problem environments show the effectiveness of our technique. In most cases of the problem instances, teams of agents were able to complete exploration of *more than* 70% of the environments. While in the *best cases*, they were able to complete explorations of *more than 80%* of the environments within short period of time. These results compare with those of Soule and Heckendorn's with performances within similar ranges. However, it is not yet clear how fair that comparison can be justified since their work employs evolutionary algorithms which come with extensive time requirements of evolutionary learning and huge time and costs of training for agents before they are deployed to actual testing environments. Our model avoids such expensive cost of extensive time requirements of evolutionary learning by agents. This is made possible as agents in our model are not subjected to training before being deployed to the testing environments. They only conduct local searches of the environments from their current locations using two important features from SLS algorithms: neighborhood and evaluation function.

We also evaluate the performance of agents' teams in another set of experiments requiring agents to search for goals in the three environments. It is interesting to note that all teams of agents were able to find on average all the goals in the three environments when the size of the grid is 12 . This is a 100% achievement by the agents' teams. However, the performance of the teams can be seen to degrade as the size of the environments becomes larger. A partial explanation for this is that since the number of agents stays the same, they need to do more work in the larger environments. These results are consistent with those based on the evaluation of agents' teams on interesting cells found in the environments. The results of these experiments suggest that the level of difficulty of the three environments are relatively the same when agents' teams implement the SLS model. This is evidenced by the closeness of the teams' average performances in the two simulations. Thus, unlike Soule and Heckendorn's evolutionary model, the SLS model's performance has *less reliance* on the three environments.

There are several areas of ongoing research on this problem. Here are some directions for future work. A drawback of Soule and Heckendorn's model is the unlimited vision of the environments by all agents in their work. We avoid this problem by ensuring that agents in our model have only limited vision of the environments except the team leader that still has unlimited vision of the environments. We plan to address this issue in future work. Our proposed SLS model in this work still has some limitations. The search approach by the model is uninformed, thus, agents exhaustively search all states by slowly branching out of their neighborhood from their starting locations. We have commenced improvement of our model by allowing agents to do more informed search of the environments by using cleverly designed and admissible heuristics to guide the search. The expectation is that agents will now have direction of the search towards the goals in the environments at every new time step.

Author details

Ramoni O. Lasisi* and Robert DuPont
Department of Computer and Information Sciences, Virginia Military Institute, United States of America

*Address all correspondence to: lasisiro@vmi.edu

References

[1] Griffiths N, Luck M. Coalition formation through motivation and trust. In: International Conference on Autonomous Agents and Multiagent Systems; Melbourne, Australia. 2003

[2] Chalkiadakis G, Elkind E, Wooldridge M. Computational Aspects of Cooperative Game Theory. California, USA: Morgan & Claypool Publishers; 2011

[3] Batalin MA, Sukhatme GS. Efficient exploration without localization. In: International Conference on Robotics and Automation; Taipei, Taiwan. 2003. pp. 2714-2719

[4] Macedo L, Cardoso A. Exploration of unknown environments with motivational agents. In: 3rd International Conference on Autonomous Agents and Multi Agent System; NYC, USA. 2004

[5] Thomason R, Heckendorn RB, Soule T. Training time and team composition robustness in evolved multi-agent systems. In: O'Neill M et al., editors. EuroGP 2008. Vol. 4971. Berlin, Heidelberg: Springer. 2008. pp. 1-12

[6] Hollinger G, Singh S, Kehagias A. Efficient, guaranteed search with multi-agent teams. In: Robotics: Science and Systems. 2009. pp. 265-272

[7] Ray DN, Majumder S, Mukhopadhyay S. A behavior-based approach for multi-agent q-learning for autonomous exploration. International Journal of Innovative Technology and Creative Engineering. 2011;**1**(7):1-15

[8] Rochlin I, Aumann Y, Sarne D, Golosman L. Efficiency fairness in team search with self-interested agents. In: 13th International Conference on Autonomous Agents and Multiagent Systems; Paris, France. 2014

[9] Okimoto T, Ribeiro T, Bouchabou D, Inoue K. Mission oriented robust multi-team formation and its application to robot rescue simulation. In: 25th International Joint Conference on Artificial Intelligence; New York City, USA. 2016

[10] Hoos HH, Stutzle T. Stochastic Local Search: Foundations and Applications. San Francisco, CA, USA: Morgan Kaufmann; 2005

[11] Neller TW. Teaching stochastic local search. In: Proceedings 19th International FLAIRS Conference on Artificial Intelligence. American Association for Artificial Intelligence. 2005:8-14

[12] Soule T, Heckendorn RB. Environmental robustness in multiagent teams. In: Genetic and Evolutionary Computation Conference; Montreal, Quebec, Canada. 2009

[13] Lasisi RO. Efficient exploration of environments using stochastic local search. In: 9th International Conference on Agents and Artificial Intelligence (ICAART 2017); Porto, Portugal. 2017. pp. 244-251

[14] Hoos HH, Stutzle T. Local search algorithms for SAT: An empirical evaluation. Journal of Automated Reasoning. 2000;**24**:421-481

[15] Russell S, Norvig P. Artificial Intelligence: A Mordern Approach. 3rd ed. New Jersey, USA: Prentice Hall; 2010